Parenthood;

How My Fathers Son Became My Sons Father

By

J.P. Morgan

Openings

So there I am, looking into my fiancé's
eyes as she is leaning towards me bent over
the side of a bed, fear etched all over her
face. My sole responsibility is to keep her
attention focused on me rather than the
imminent pain she is about to endure.
However I cannot help but notice the
enormous mountain of a man who is
positioning himself directly behind her. He
smiles and winks at me as he informs us both
reassuringly that 'It's going in nicely
now….'

Now if you find any of that even the
slightest bit erotic I think you may have
picked up the wrong book. However if you

have ever found yourself overwhelmed in a crowded room of a maternity hospital thinking to yourself 'That pregnancy book was *way* off!' then you just might enjoy reading a little further.

You see when it comes to preparation for parenthood you are never short of incoming advice on what to expect. You listen intently to friends, parents and siblings who are usually more than happy to chip in their two cents on what having your own children will be like. As expectant parents you will also find yourself presented with or purchasing several parenting books, each with their own unique academic take on parenting perfection. So in theory you should be fully prepared. Unfortunately the fact is that no book and no-one will ever be able to fully prepare you for the rollercoaster ride that is pregnancy. Not to mention the night of the delivery and what follows in the weeks, months and years ahead. And I believe that's actually a good thing, a great thing in fact. Because by learning from scratch, on the job as it were, you get to create your own experience without prejudice or comparison to anyone else's story. And that experience could be what comes to define your life's work when you look back many years from now to that night you met your first born child. No pressure at all then.

My own journey from being my fathers' son to becoming my sons' father has raised many questions and I'm still searching for most of the answers. As I speak to my own parents and my peers I realise that a lot of my questions are pretty common. They speak to our universal need to understand what it is to be a parent, either as you reminisce about your own folks or are embarking on the grand journey for yourself. This book is my attempt to at least ask some of those big questions if not always coming up with the right answers. Luckily I've had plenty of input from family, friends and random parents as they shuffle around their local playground never more than two feet behind their tottering toddlers. Their answers, comments and stories pop up throughout this book highlighted in *"text that looks like this"*

So what kind of questions are you getting yourself in for? Well you probably won't find them in any of the traditional pregnancy or parenting books. They are also the reason I don't get invited to many dinner parties anymore. That's because I love asking the big awkward questions, though I have to admit that my timing is not always the best. For example, very few things tend to bring Christmas dinner to an uncomfortable halt like 'Mam, where did I come from? I mean, I know you love me but...did you actually want or plan for me...considering you were 42 at the time??...Oh and pass the mushy peas while you're mulling that over thanks a mill'

Like a toddler stuck in the habit of asking *why* to everything all day long I just never stop wondering. What kind of baby was I? Did you really dip my soother in whiskey before resting me in my lead paint-coated cot? What toys did I like? Why did you let me watch Chitty Chitty Bang Bang alone, I mean, have you *seen* the child catcher bit?? How bad a teenager was I? Was it obvious when I starting smoking & drinking or did I get away with it like the shifty chameleon I imagined I was? Did you ever believe I would get married? Will I be a good Dad? How did you make it look so easy?

Since I subsequently began my own odyssey into the realms of Parenthood the volume of questions has only increased. Why can I not seem to do anything right during first and third trimester of pregnancy? Am I actually being of any help during this delivery or is the nurse patronising me? Arguably my favourite is; *why* do nurses and doctors think its okay to allow two completely inexperienced people to leave a hospital with a tiny baby!

These days you can't adopt a puppy without rigorous home and background checks but removing a new born infant from a medical facility is apparently no more difficult than renting a DVD. That's obviously providing you show at least *some* interest in the baby and display a little awareness of the basic need to securely strap a baby into a car-seat. But before you know it you are home. Closing the front door behind you then turning to see a tiny pair of eyes peeking out from under a mountain of blankets. You all have the same awestruck yet puzzled look on your face. Both parents and baby are hoping the stranger facing them will miraculously develop telepathic abilities and figure out what they want to say to each other. The majority of us who have found ourselves in that exact moment after arriving home would secretly admit that we were all thinking the same thing…What the hell are we supposed to do now?! There is no universal answer. We each just figure it out for ourselves. One of only two crumbs of advice this book will offer is to simply be visible and wait. The next thing you do will involve either a nappy, food or a blanket…possibly all three. It's easy for me to say this now of course since we have been through it a couple of times. I still recall it as both a thrilling and daunting prospect though. Just be sure to stick the kettle on, there is no such thing as an Irish situation that isn't made easier by a cup of tea.

The questions confronting parents today don't necessarily get any easier with experience. Some are soul-destroying on a daily basis, like where has the fabled 'property ladder' gone and how come no one is allowed to climb it anymore? Thankfully our kids can provide the distraction required to keep us plugging away during recessionary times. In other words, it's difficult to focus on the economy whilst wondering aloud to yourself 'why on earth does my son like to drink out of puddles like a dog?' Arguably the most important question of all will always be 'Am I a good parent?' Let's come back to that one later.

Ultimately though, what I have enjoyed most about working on this book is hearing so many different perspectives on parenting. What I have realised is just how many things are constant when it comes to parenting, regardless of your race, religion or country of origin. Some basic traits will almost always come to pass, whether you like it or not. Your parents will shower you with guilt for the torment you caused them as a child and only occasionally sprinkle it with words of praise. Your kids will gradually move through phases where they first idolise you and then simply love you. Next they may just about like you before they are barely able to tolerate you. All the while they will use that tolerance to facilitate borrowing money from you. Eventually they will end up hating you for no apparent reason and ultimately leave you. But hopefully one day they will come back to you. And when they do you will complete the circle by drowning them in guilt until they deliver the reward you've been waiting for since the first day you laid eyes on them, Grandchildren!

Oh and don't worry, I will be returning to the saucy tale of the giant male nurse and my fiancé a little later. It gets even steamier when we are joined by three more nurses, a snooty consultant and we all take a good long look at my future wife's vagina.

I must have missed the chapter in the books that supposed to adequately prepare you for that situation.

However I am relieved neither of our mothers had a go at preparing us for it either. That discussion would most likely have included too many hand actions, some holy water and at least one reference to a manger in Bethlehem.

One

Of a Saturday Morning...

"You're going to eat that dinner, and you're going to enjoy it whether you like it or not!"

- Brian, Father of Five.

Being a parent is hard. Who in their right mind would apply for a job that pays no salary and requires 24 hours shifts? It's a lifetime of worry and frustration with zero guarantee of success or gratitude. The requirement to become an instant expert on the colour, consistency and content of someone else's poo is also a significant drawback. Why do we do it if it is so hard? Does something instinctive compel us into paternal & maternal roles despite the fact we know they are so difficult a role to fulfil. But then again so is the role of being a kid. You are unable to defend yourself from innocuous illnesses and constantly require another person to help you complete routine tasks. It seems to take forever for your limbs and brain to work in a co-ordinated fashion. Worst of all the giant apes standing around you, who appear to be in charge, have no idea how to communicate with you at all…and that's all just when you're a teenager!

It's one of the most universal ironies we ever encounter in our lives. We are born, raised & educated by men & women who we subsequently spend a significant portion of our lives failing to understand. The real kicker is that, in general, the vast majority of us will find ourselves filling

the very position of authority &
responsibility we spent so long trying to
emancipate ourselves from. It seems that
even those apples that fall some distance
from the tree can always find a way of
rolling back under those familiar welcoming
branches.

In theory, becoming a parent should be a
doddle because you get anywhere from one to
two decades of 'on the job' tutelage simply
by being the child of your own Mam & Dad.
And yet, as with your parents before you,
nothing will ever truly prepare you for the
challenges & triumphs, disappointments &
ecstasy that await you. You just have to
play it by ear as a wise man is so fond of
telling me.

That wise man is my Dad. And when it comes
to understanding the highs & lows of

childhood and the perpetually unwinnable position of a parent where better to start than with my own parents.

Now, if you are looking for the exact date of my parents wedding or the song that they first danced together to you are in the wrong place. Those details and memories are not my domain. Besides if you want to know more about that kind of stuff about them all you have to do is ask them yourself. Just be sure to pour a strong cup of tea for my Dad and a stronger Bacardi for Mam and they'll regale you with every last detail you need. However what *I* can share is what it was like to be their son; to turn to them for advice, to occasionally make them proud and unfortunately quite often disappoint them. In other words, my parents memoirs will tell you their journey whilst my perspective will tell you how they shaped me first as a child and ultimately as a parent myself.

With regards to my folks it's actually quite difficult & overwhelming for me to attempt to describe their respective characters. Especially when all the people and events that made them the parents I was born to in August of '78 had already happened long before I arrived on the planet!

Let me ease in to this with some adjectives that spring to mind when I think firstly about my father. 'Constant' is one, his middle name could actually be 'Northern Star' such is his dependability. Pick any day of the year, any time of day and any topic at all you want to talk about. I guarantee you my Dad will greet you like an overdue sunrise, listen intently to you, and provide logical sound advice before sending you on your way with a gentle hug & wistful wave.

'Kind' is another word that comes to mind, generous to a fault at times in fact. Time and again he puts his own motivations and desires behind those of others. Always kind in his actions and he has never been known to turn down a request for any kind of help, be it a lift to work or help with DIY. But perhaps even more importantly the kindness exuded by his thoughts and words. Often he has found himself in the midst of conflict that was not of his own making. The easy thing to do would be to take sides and/or belittle one party to gain the confidence of another. Seeing the real damage that conflict can do in his own past, he has chosen instead to be resolutely steadfast in his opposition to conflict. He instead uses whatever influence he can muster to encourage all sides to find a common ground and move on.

Finally on adjective side of things, the word that I cannot avoid is 'Husband'. Yes I know that it's *technically* not an adjective but it does help us link the man to his better half quite nicely. Whilst to me he will always be simply Dad, I know to my Mam he is so much more than that. To forge a marriage that lasts over half a century brings five children and subsequently eight grandchildren into the world takes two singular people destined to make each other whole. On the surface one could say in terms of The Morgan Family that my Mam is the heart & my Dad is the brain but that does a disservice to both of them. My Mam may be

the outwardly emotional yang to my Dads
internalising yin but even the strongest
hurricane of activity requires a solid calm
Eye to exist. My Dad makes my Mam more than
she could ever be alone but he knows (as we
all do) that she does the exactly the same
for him. All their associated off-spring
(myself included) have benefited from this
synergy. We rarely manage to shy away from
the limelight socially (for better or worse)
but are always willing to offer a kind ear
that anyone who needs our support. We
neither spontaneously obtained those traits
nor licked them off the stones. In short,
just as I could not exist without both my
parents input (poor choice of words sorry),
I also realise that they could not exist
without each other. There's a reason my Mam
gave him a second chance after he stood her
up on their first date. Though I doubt it

was because he sang poetry through yonder window to her.

For you see, despite being an accomplished public speaker my Dad has never been much of a talker…in the touchy-feely sense of the word I mean. In day to day terms he could talk for Ireland though. He will talk the hind legs off a donkey on the ins & outs of electrical switchboards and how many kilowatt hours your time in the shower costs. He frequently regales us with the latest number of cygnets killed off by foxes in the local park as we walk by the lake during the summer months. But when it comes to matters of the heart and more emotive conversations he tends to keep his own counsel, retaining his stoic composure throughout. I understand now that has never been due to any lack of compassion or

affection towards me or my siblings. Quite
the opposite in fact, he just finds other
ways to communicate the love and pride he
feels for his family.

One of the ways I remember being literally
sweeter than others was every Friday evening
when I was no more than 7 or 8 years old. He
would arrive home from work with a wrinkled
brown paper bag under his arm. I would be
leaping at the front door as he walked up
the driveway such was my excitement. Once he
reached the living room he would unveil the
bounty from within the bag. He wouldn't just
fling one at me however. A full bar would
not be appropriate for a growing boy. I
understood that and knew the routine. He
would open his favourite bar, Fry's Mint
Chocolate, and break off half of it for me.
After handing it to me he would turn to take

a seat in the armchair before looking back to see nothing but a chocolate smudge where my mouth used to be. I would wolf down the bar before he could even start his 'Now take your time with that…' speech. The first in a long line of disappointments I my big mouth caused him.

Even further back down memory lane is the shared Saturday morning activity which formed the foundation of our relationship. Given the importance my Dad places on the activity I'm sure it's an experience my brothers & sisters can attest to also. I speak of course of the ancient art of swimming. I love swimming and it's something we introduced to both my own sons as soon as they could kick their legs. But let me clarify something, I love swimming *now*. Back then on those Saturday mornings it was torturous. Spluttering around the pool being shouted at for clinging to the ropes while my Dad sat watching from the stands is still the stuff of my nightmares. I hated that hour in the pool so much at the time that the anxiety used to make me physically sick, before an during the swim.

But looking back I now realise two important things. Firstly, I know that every unexpected mouthful of chlorine-laced water I swallowed in my formative years gave me the confidence to continue to swim throughout the rest of my life. Any chance I get be it in the local leisure centre, on holidays or in the sea. Moreover I get the chance to begin the whole learning process again with my own children. And as a result I am eternally grateful to my father for introducing me to swimming and pushing me past my own awkward reluctance.

Secondly, and far more importantly, those 60 terrifying minutes spent in the pool are not what I remember most. What I remember now is the giddy feeling of being allowed sit in the front seat of my Dad's car (Health & Safety hadn't been invented yet) on route to the pool in Ringsend. I remember the canal flashing past us on the left, laden with more litter than ducklings. I remember Sinatra and his 'Doo-be-Doo-be-Doo' emanating effortlessly from the tape deck as we took the blind right turn from Harold's Cross and made our way past countless bridges & locks. I remember counting each of set of lights and just wishing there was always another one left so my Dad & I could spend just a few minutes more in that tranquil setting before heading for the changing rooms. Then yes to be fair the tranquillity was replaced by blind panic once the pool came into view. The panic only escalated from there too. Firstly due to being forced to wear Speedos in public before you have grown the requisite 'twig & berries' to appropriately fill them. And secondly by being literally thrown into a freezing cold pool as that very action was being referred to as 'Lesson 1'!

However, once the trauma of the hour long 'swimming lesson' was over I would race up the stairs of the leisure centre, leaping two steps at a time so as to reach the lounge bar as quick as my little legs would get me there. Why the sudden change in demeanour? Because there, in the lounge waiting for me, would be my reward for managing to stay afloat while swallowing my own body weight in water for the previous hour in the pool. There, like a homecoming feast to a returning soldier, would be the highlight of my week. A tall, slender glass of fizzy orange and a chilled bar of chocolate, a KitKat usually. After a week of stew, coddle and casserole for lunch & dinner, which were all actually the same food just poured from different pots, this was a real treat. I was in heaven. The best was still yet to come too as a fluorescent light flickered to life over the small sized snooker table in the corner of the bar. I would race over as my Dad would amble behind me and we would play a few frames of snooker. Well, I say we played but the *play* mostly consisted of my Dad explaining the rules and telling me to 'take my time'. He didn't seem to care that I could barely see over the rim of the table let alone control the cue!

Those mornings were so simple and yet remain the cornerstone of my relationship with my Dad. What I once considered simply mundane things like music on the car stereo, a bar of chocolate and a never-ending frame of snooker have become something far more important when viewed through the prism of raising my own children. What he gave me was simply time. He worked every hour God sent during the week and the first thing he did on the weekend was to take me out all morning. True I did nearly drown on more than one occasion but it was priceless father & son time nonetheless.

This unfortunately makes me so regretful that I wasted so many of my teenage years resenting the man as I passed painfully through puberty. I was so certain he was out of touch with reality and I now had all the answers. Sure he was just a strict disciplinarian who knew nothing about *my* modern world, wasn't he? Yep, I was a teenager and to my shame it cost me many years of friendship & guidance from my parents especially my Dad. Will my boys really turn on me in the same fashion I once did to their Granddad? But I spend even more time with them than my Dad was able to with me…surely this time it will be different?

Sometimes we delude ourselves into thinking that with us it will be different. We will be the first truly *cool* parents in human history and we will never be rebelled against. Never be shouted at or kept in the dark about girls, alcohol or worse. We will be the cool parents who are Facebook friends with our kids and even closer friends in the real world. These delusions are of course the steamiest variety of horseshit available on the market today.

We will be just as cool and accessible as our parents were and their parents were before them, that is to say, not at all. For a few years at least we will be the very epitome of authority and as a result we will be despised by our kids. We just have to hope we handle it well enough and let them storm out of the nest in such a way that they know they can always fly back to us when they are ready. We hope. It took me the best part of a decade to fly back to the nest and it's very difficult for us to contemplate losing real contact with the boys for that long. But we most likely will do exactly that if their own parents' teenage journeys are any indication of future behaviours. I was an unbridled arsehole to my folks as a teenager and it seems inevitable my boys will prove to me that what goes around comes around.

So what stopped the rot & made me realise how wrong I was treating them? Well as Shakespeare once wrote 'I eventually pulled my head out of my arse'. And I can remember the exact point in time at which that happened. It was November 1997, the night my Dad retired from the ESB.

But before I get to that pivotal moment, I want to be sure that I'm not painting too grim a picture here. I was not a complete 'juvenile delinquent' (despite being called that on more than one occasion) by any stretch of the imagination. I never really strayed *too* far from the straight & narrow for too long. To be honest I was about average on the scale of teenage angst & rebellion. There were plenty of times in fact when my parents wished I would stray very far away from them indeed! Ask and they will recall with eyes rolled to Heaven about a holiday in Majorca when I was ten and for the entire two weeks I barely wandered more two feet from my mother's side. I was very timid and to make matters worse there was a young Scottish lass in the same holiday complex who apparently had an eye for the 'wee shy lad from Dublin'. A persistent offer of friendship that involved lots of 'heavy petting' throughout the holiday only triggered the exact opposite reaction that she and my parents would have hoped for. In short if I could have perched atop my fathers head for the remainder of the trip I gladly would have. I vividly remember the confused & dazed look on their faces when I ran to them telling them 'she was trying to touch me under the water in the pool'. My Mam admirably comforted me and told me to stay away from the buxom Scot even if she wished secretly I was a little more mature. My Dad's external reaction was nil. Inside I can only imagine he was shouting 'Get back in the pool and take one for the team, we're sick of you!'

So yes I was very much a late bloomer. It wasn't until the age of 12 or 13 that I started to chisel out my own identity which gradually fostered more independence and distance from my parents, especially Dad. But while I was never a complete tearaway what I most definitely rebelled against was my parent's position of moral and intellectual authority. Whether it was

programming the video recorder or drinking &
smoking at 15 I knew it all and their input
was not required. Their very existence was
almost little more than a hindrance to my
unbridled ascent into adulthood and world
domination. I say 'almost' because how can a
superhuman entity such as an entitled
teenager conquer the world without his
Father giving him 20 quid to cover the cost
of the night out!

The worst moment of this ridiculous period
which sticks most in the memory involves
swimming (of course it involves swimming.
Seriously, my childhood should have put me
off swimming as much as Jaws did for
everyone else!). It was a Sunday afternoon
and in the absence of any other valuable
interests I was encouraged by my father to
get ready to go for a family swim. A family

swim? Did he know who he was talking to? I was my own man, I did what I wanted when I wanted to do it so I did what every world class teenager would do in that situation, I began to complain. A little huffing and puffing first to set the mood before stomping the feet and muttering, I really did have it down to a fine art. So it was time to close the sale and at the top of the stars I started into my spoiled whiny anthem of hating swimming and hating my parents and then BANG!

Before I knew what had happened my feet were off the ground and I was pinned by the throat against the exterior wall of the bathroom at the top of the stairs. My father, the diplomat the quiet man, had me by the neck and wasn't letting go. It wasn't a thrashing but I didn't budge (not that I could anyway). He leaned towards me and as matter-a-fact as if he was talking about the weather he said 'Now, you are going swimming and you are going to enjoy…whether you like it or not'. I don't recall exactly what I felt at that moment other than fear mixed with submission. What I do know is the only noise I could muster to pass my lips was 'Yes'. I took my punishment and went swimming but remained simmering and entitled for a few more years never too far from throwing a tantrum whenever I was challenged at home. I strategically only acted up when it was just my Mam who was home though, I wasn't *that* stupid.

What causes me even more regret looking back is the fact that outside the remit of my parents, in the outside world, I was really coming into my own. I had plenty of friends and was generally always inclined towards doing the right & noble thing for those around me. It's ironic to look back now realising that I was making a name for myself as a good (young) man and it was a direct result of how I had been raised by my parents. And I didn't even realise it because when I got home I was too busy hating them for no apparent reason. Well thankfully that was about to come to a long overdue and bittersweet end in November 1997.

It was the night of my Dad's retirement party to celebrate leaving the ESB after four and a half decades of loyal service. It should be noted that this would turn out to be his last retirement party but not his last retirement. Brian Morgan has proved more difficult to remove from the workforce

than it is to get the late great James Brown
off stage at the end of a gig. He's had more
comebacks than Rocky Balboa at this stage
and he's not finished yet.

So there I was, 19 years of age, working
part-time and studying in college, a man in
my own eyes but suddenly feeling adrift in a
function room full of real men & women.
People with actual life experience who had
been there and failed and got up again and
then succeeded. They had created jobs,
raised families, and built companies,
survived recessions, depressions & Sonny
Knowles. Here I was an upstart, an invisible
irrelevance, in a room of giants. And then
it hit me. Like a kick in the pit of my
stomach it hit me. These men & women, these
relative giants were all here for my Dad.
There was a swirling air of respect,

admiration, self-less joy and love moistening the room and it was all flooding towards my parents. They were all there to celebrate my Dad and his wife. Having suddenly realised this I became overwhelmed with one undeniably powerful and gut-wrenching emotion, shame.

I will never forget the next question that I asked myself…'who the f*ck do you think you are?!' These people with all their varying skills, experience and accomplishments were there celebrating my father and they only worked with him. I was *raised* by him and I thought *I* was a better man? I knew it all and he was a **hindrance**?? I didn't deserve to be drinking the free beer in my hand. Free beer that was now tasting more and more bitter by the moment. By the time I surrendered the glass to the nearest table my mouth felt like I had been sipping a fluid akin to cod liver oil laced with thumb tacks. I didn't deserve to be in that room. Worst of all I knew my Dad deserved a better son than I had been to him. I slinked out of that room alone after painfully wishing my parents a happy night in a hollow gesture knowing I had no right to wish them anything whatsoever. On the journey home I swore to myself that I would never again forsake my Mam & Dad. Moreover I would spend every day for the rest of my life & theirs earning the right to be proud to be their son and ensuring they knew I loved them dearly. In short, as I said, on that bittersweet night I finally decided to take my head out of my arse.

Still with me? Good, because it wasn't all angst-ridden gloom. One of the many bright points that endured during those moody teenager years was another of my parents' great passions and gifts to me. Golf. I must have been 14 or 15 when they first started encouraging me to play. This encouragement allowed me one of the first glimpses into my Dads mischievous side which he had always hidden so well as I grew up. He knew I was neither capable nor worthy of my own set of clubs the first few times he took me out on a golf course. So I guess his way of testing my interest in the game without wasting money on clubs or green fees was to present me as his playful caddy. I was just along with my folks to help out and nothing more. Then when we got far enough out of sight from the clubhouse Dad would hand me a club and drop a pristine golf ball onto the lush fairway in front of me. I cannot describe how exhilarating this was for me the first time it happened which was on a pokey little woodlands course in Charleville during a summer holiday in County Cork in 1993. Not just because I was a hormone-riddled teenager being handed a metal stick and actually encouraged to hit something with it. More importantly, my Dad, the quintessential gentleman, was breaking the rules…for me.

From that point on I was hooked and played golf with my Mam & Dad around once a month for the next few years. There were still plenty of mood-related mishaps along the way. Particularly as my father tried to coach me on not just the mechanics of the game but also the decorum involved. On the morning of a game I would be fascinated watching him out the kitchen window practicing his elegant steady metronomic swing. Naturally he would never dream of practicing his golf swing on the pristine lawn out the back which resembled the pitch in Wembley *before* anyone had ever played on it. So he ingeniously used a slender doormat from which to chip & strike the numerous plastic practice golf balls he had. He always encouraged me to practice as often as possible which I resented initially because it felt like a school lesson but after a while he would leave me to practice on my own and that's when the fun started.

The 'safety' mat was quickly discarded. The plastic practice golf balls swiftly dwindled in number as I thrashed at the lawn like apprentice butcher eagerly testing his first meat cleaver. Within 23 minutes of my imaginary Ryder Cup campaign around the back garden all of the plastic golf balls were in a different garden and the lawn looked more like Lansdowne Road than Wembley. I decided to head to the club house and invent an appropriate cover story for the damage & loss incurred. But since (until now) my Dad was unaware of the carnage I thought I could just edge one final step further away from the structured format with which the lesson began when I caught sight of a shiny new Maxfli golf ball. One from his personal stash no doubt, he must have forgotten about it after he finished practicing a few chips. So with a quick scan of the back windows of the house for anyone watching, I placed the ball on the lush green grass, aimed very roughly away from the back of the house, grabbed the heaviest club I could find and swung like Babe Ruth...

To this day I have no idea where that ball went but I know those impromptu coaching sessions gradually became a little more mature the more I learnt from my father about the simplicity of the game. When we played together I would be imagining myself in the same league as Nick Faldo. I would need to consider the grain of the fairway, changes in elevation, subtle wind alterations, the speed of the green and probably the impact of the full moon on low tide for good measure. And as a result I would have complicated things so much in my mind that I would end up removing a sizeable chunk of muck with my club and sending the ball bobbling a few yards to the left. At which point Dad would step in like some Buddhist spirit guide and proceed to clear my mind of everything bar a few simple words. Keep your head still, Don't bend your elbow and swing slow. CRACK is the next sound heard as the ball flew in the general direction of the shorter grass.

And that in a nutshell is how he has always imparted his life affirming & life changing advice to me regardless of the situation it always revolves around simplicity & calm...

"Keep your head, Don't panic & Take your time..."

And I guess one could say he and his sagely advice have helped me to keep my life heading in the general direction of the short grass.

To this very day the irony never escapes me when I hear phrases like 'calm down, relax & think' or 'Who left the television on in here with no-one watching it?' coming out of my own mouth. I always afford myself a rye smile when I realise that despite nearly a decade pretending I would be anything other than similar to my own parents I ended up an almost identical chip of the old blocks. The smile strengthens when I think of how lucky I am to have had folks like mine and of how my inherited skills should in turn bode well for my own kids.

And then all of a sudden a daunting prospect floats in amongst my thoughts. It dawns on me that, regardless of how attentive or cool a parent I might think I am, there is pretty much a cast iron guarantee that I will be sentenced to ten years of hatred & acrimony by my sons when they reach puberty. It doesn't matter if I have an iPad and a million Facebook friends they will turn their backs on us for close to a decade at least. We just have to hang in there and hope we put enough good stuff in the tank before then to ensure they eventually have a realisation like their Dad did at the end of his teenage years. Either way there is even a more daunting prospect to consider. What do you do on the day that they realise or decide that they no longer need you? How do you possibly begin to trust them to do the right thing when you are no longer by their side to guide them? How can they cope in the big bad world on their own and possibly be safe…without you by their side…

———————————————

Two

Letting Go...A Little.

"I sit and watch my 2 boys, one by one, mount the stage in the impressive O'Reilly hall in UCD and receive their prize from the school principal. An achievement prize for each, awarded to the top performers in each year. They don't look very much alike, but they grin in exactly the same way, half proud, half embarrassed, and slouch back to their seats in that careless, nonchalant teenage way.

If I close my eyes I can remember.....the days when I carried both, one on each arm, up the front steps to their crèche. Every morning thinking....if only they could both walk up beside me, how much easier my morning drop-off would be. ...

I stand by the soccer field in Dalkey, another freezing Sunday morning. I watch my older boy playing his heart out, captain of his team, urging his team mates on, and they come back and win the game, having been 2 nil down at half time. I am hoarse from cheering them on. And we drive home, analysing the game and the opposition, and he is on top of the World after his victory.

And if I close my eyes I can remember the shy little 5 year old boy, who had to be coaxed from the car in the suburbs of Chicago, to join his new soccer team at the local YMCA.

Again on the side-line, this time a rugby pitch, watching my younger son lining up in the second row. He glances over at me, and I point at my head. He rolls his eyes, but jogs back to the side line and pulls on his scrum cap. He grins at me and crouches down with his classmates in the scrum, this big strong boy, at 14 already taller than me. And again I remember, the day after he was born, when the paediatrician doing her rounds in the maternity hospital, checking all the new-born's. And after listening to his heart she frowns. And watching her, my own heart stops as I ask 'Is something wrong?' 'I am just going to have another listen' she says, and time seems to stand still as she focuses her attention on the little squirming chest under her stethoscope. She straightens up then and said 'No, all fine' ....and I can breathe again.

They are without doubt my proudest achievement. My degree, my masters, my own personal career accomplishments, nothing makes me as proud as I am of my boys. And nothing wounds me as much as their hurts, their disappointments."

- Eileen, Mum of Two

In contrast to my Dads steady driving force pushing me forwards in a structured manner there was always my Mam. Filling me with hope & optimism that I could push even further and become anything I wanted. Sincere always, even if not always entirely truthful…

"Don't be silly, I've seen the lads in your class and you are more handsome than any of them…"

I'm no looker now and at the age of 12 I was even less alluring so she was a little off the mark there. She probably knew it too. But her motivations were always true to that form, filling me with confidence and self-belief was all she ever tried to do. I am extremely grateful for that now but the shock of finding out that girls of my age at that time did not share my mother's glowing opinion of me was more than a little disappointing. Pre-teen discos were a particularly remorseless battleground for meek young boys like me. And they were the scene of some of the harshest wounds which I suffered at the hands of the fairer sex. The repetitive no's they responded to my romantic advances with were bad enough. But worse still was when a friend would approach a girl on my behalf. I would see him motion towards me as I tried to look casual, cool and pretending I knew how to dance. I would sop swaying side to side just long enough to see him skulk back in my direction. Behind him usually was a gaggle of giggling girls pointing and shaking their heads…

"Well, what did she say???"

"Do you really want to know?"

"....Eh no, maybe not...(*devastated exhale*)...ok...Who's next?"

Due to my Mam's constant support and belief I never gave up. The night of my first kiss was just such an example of the fact that I never accepted 'feck off' for an answer. I asked 27 girls if they would like to dance with me and received 27 straight impolite no's. But whether it was pity, lack of options or just blind luck number 28 finally said yes and I smooched her like a mule eating an apple. She had braces but it made no difference to me. She could have been wearing a bridle and answered to the name Shergar and I wouldn't have stopped. I was 'meeting' a girl and that's all that mattered. I don't know what they call it nowadays but I'm pretty sure it's not referred to as 'Will ye meet me mate?' I doubt it stops at kissing either but that's a can of worms we'll get to pop open later.

I would be lying if I said I was thinking of my Mam at that exact moment…and probably a little disturbed too come to think of it. But I see now that my ridiculously cavalier attitude towards believing in myself stemmed straight from my Mam's belief in me, and it still does. She believes in all her children and grandchildren. The trouble is, like many women of her generation, she has little belief in herself. She is always her own worst critic and remembers almost nothing but the mistakes she thinks she has made in her life. Since I was born in the year of her 42nd birthday it is most likely that I was one of those mistakes. But she loved me and filled me full of as much self-belief as she could so that in time she could in turn do the most difficult thing any mother ever has to contemplate. She had to let me go. Though, at times, it was not the most difficult decision for her as it might have been. During my worst phases of adult childishness, she wasn't so much thinking that maybe it was time for me to move out as physically pushing me out of the nest not caring whether my wings were ready or not!

In general, the most appropriate time and manner in which to start allowing your child to be a little more independent seemingly appears to differ depending on gender. I have to be very careful with my choice of words but *in general* Dad's like to encourage increasing levels of independence a lot sooner than Mum is comfortable with. This can (and will) cause friction at times. Dads tend to switch to 'hunter gatherer' mode and expect the child to fend for themselves and move out by their third birthday. Meanwhile Mom's will want to cradle, swaddle and do everything for them even as their 'baby' is putting on the suit for their wedding day.

My Mam was most definitely a member of that latter category. In her heart anyway, I think by the time I headed into my late teens & early twenties she was ready to sever those apron strings like she was chopping away the rotten tip of an otherwise healthy carrot. This was not because she was callous or uncaring in any way, quite the opposite, even now to this very day. But by the time I was supposedly becoming a man in my own right my folks were in their mid-sixties. They were focusing on enjoying their first four grandchildren and reducing their golf handicaps. After raising four children already and escorting them into independent adulthood they were not too worried about swaddling their youngest child for much longer. I was showing signs of being ready to move on whilst they were most definitely ready to enjoy their well-deserved retirement from full-time parenting. And so after the briefest of periods I moved out and into my own place just after my 21st birthday. Yes I admit that technically, if you used a traditional calendar, it was actually just *8 years* after. The trouble is that Dads will never fully understand (or abide) the strength of the bond between a mother & her child. Even when both sides are in complete agreement on the need to induce independence one way or another, mothers will always flinch at the last minute. Something which has kept many an Irish son at home a lot longer than was necessary or financially viable.

There are many factors at play here on all sides. Dad not only has the instinctual need to drive his offspring into an independent state as soon as possible. It is also just easier for Dad to divorce himself from any emotional attachment and focus on the practical side of child rearing. It's a disposition some fathers welcome whilst others have it thrust upon them. We do not have the same physical bond that mothers do because we are not the ones who are anatomically designed to carry and give birth to our offspring. If we were seahorses it might be different but something tells me Daddy seahorses still end up agreeing with their birth partners as much as we human fathers do. It's just good biological practice in all walks of life.

We are mostly innocent bystanders during the most crucial phase of child & parent bonding. Dads can do their best to reduce stress levels on both mother & child with the occasional backrub or prepared meal. However, the best intentions will still almost inevitably end up causing a tearful & irrational shouting match over something neither party actually cares about. Unfortunately for Dads the same result is encountered even if they hedge their bets and focus on doing nothing at all to avoid doing something wrong entirely. All you can do is try to help as best you can. Then be sure to follow up that effort with an understanding that the torrent of abuse you receive for delivering a cup of tea a single degree too hot (or cold) is neither intended for you nor your fault. You just happened to be in the *right* place at the *right* time.

So while Mum develops all sorts of connections with her baby Dad has to pretend he gets it while feeling somewhat isolated from the experience. Upon arrival baby will cling to mother and the automatic emotional imprinting begins anew. Regardless of how close & attentive Dad might be the relationship never reaches the same heights of symbiosis. Within a few days there's a good chance Dad will be heading back to work leaving mother & child to bond further as they become accustomed to the new routine of living together. Dad will see life return to normal in many ways and as a result can sometimes be already looking for ways to restore said normalcy in the home without realising that not everyone is on the same page as him.

And it's from those unspoken roots that many arguments will sprout over the following couple of decades. Mum will look to hold on to and sometimes spoil their *baby* while Dad will be holding the front door open accompanied by not so gentle words of encouragement to their under achieving man-child. The truth is it doesn't matter which position you take. Independence cannot be injected into your offspring any more than charisma or sex appeal can. It comes from within and can be fostered by providing a decent balance of the baby / man-child approaches. Whether you wish the day will never come or not it is pretty much guaranteed that it will and when it does it will probably blind-side you and you won't know how to react.

I'll never forget my Mam's reaction to my declaration that I was getting ready to stretch my wings and leave the comfort of her nest. I knew by this point in time, the ripe old age of 27, I was ready to go. I knew they both wanted & needed me to go for financial reasons and several other reasons they could file under 'miscellaneous'. 45 minute long (electric!) showers were not something my Dad was happy with to say the least. Every time I stepped out of the bathroom accompanied by a tsunami of steam I was educated in the number of kilowatt hours I had just consumed and how much it had cost. My entertainment preferences were simply & wholly incompatible with my folks and my eldest sister. The remote control for the TV became prime real estate which was fought over with fierce territoriality. Not that it mattered all that much because regardless of where I hid the remote after sticking on an episode of The Simpsons my Dad wouldn't have to go looking for it. I would get it for him and place it in his hand. Why? Because he told me to, in that inimitable direct manner that was never to be trifled with. A decade had passed since he had me up against that wall, feet off the ground. I was now a fraction taller than him but my physical stature accounted for little in terms of debate. He still held complete authority over me whenever he needed to assert it. What was running out was his patience as it was for my Mam & sister…

"Is there milk for a cup of tea? Where is the bread for lunch? Where's my bar of chocolate I hid away where no-one could find it?"

Where? The same place every natural resource in the house went. It was hoovered up by the man-child. It was time for a change for all of us. And my Mam received the news in typically frantic but ultimately acquiescent fashion...

"-Mam, I've something to tell you..."

"...(*eyebrows furrow, hands wring*)...Jesus Mary & Joseph...Are you on drugs?"

"No!"

"...You're gay aren't you? Jesus I knew it"

"No, I'm not gay, will you let me fin-"

"...Who's pregnant? Who is she? I'll box your ears now tell me?"

"Mam, nothings wrong, I just-wait, why did you assume I was gay before pregnant?-anyway it doesn't matter. What I'm trying to say is I want to move out and leave home...Mam?....You ok?....its just for a while at first like, ye know, travel a bit that's all, I'll be back before you know it"

"…(*relaxed exhale*)…Well at least I know your not on drugs, c'mere, give us a hug"

Compared to…

"-Dad? Can I tell you something"

"Go ahead"

"I'm leaving home…for a while at least"

"That's smashin' kiddo, well done!"

I know they both loved me but equally I'm sure they were both washed over by a mixture of pride, relief and a slight dose of 'it's about feckin time!'

And so I spread my wings a little and left home for a few months to see what it was like beyond the borders of the nest. Never being one to stray to far from tradition I travelled to Australia and New Zealand. Like most Irish people there were a few long settled relations dotted around the continent to I was never too far from a friendly face. But the journey served its purpose well. Within a few days of returning home it was obvious to me that the itch of independent living could not be scratched from under 'Mammys wing'. So I began the process of moving out permanently and purchased my own place a few months later. If you are following this story in chronological order you will deduce that my decision to buy a property occurred in early 2007. The ink was not even dry on my signature for the mortgage before the rumblings of storm clouds began to be heard. Like so many fledgling homeowners in Ireland I am still living with the consequences of my decision and the decisions of other more well-paid people I have never met. More on that later.

I'm sure there were some mixed feelings on my parent's side with regards to my departure but they never let them show. In fact they were so intent on not letting me see how upset they were with their youngest child flying the coop that they promptly remodelled my room into an office / extra wardrobe space within days of my departure. How very considerate of them to spare my feelings with such nobility and stiffness of upper lip…though they might have at least had a days wake for me before ripping up the carpet! After 29 years under their roof I walked out for the last time (as a lodger anyway) on a sunny Saturday afternoon. My Mam was away with her pitch & putt club and my Dad barely turned his gaze away from the 6-nation's rugby match being televised that day to say goodbye. Not the most auspicious circumstances for such a momentous day I thought. But maybe they knew I'd be back before too long. They were right; I returned within two hours and took a lasagne from the freezer.

When I compare my own mother to the new mothers I meet today the majority of the basic maternal instincts I remember (and took advantage of) in her remain visible in others today. However, if there is one positive progressive change in the mindset of the 'Irish Mammy' over the last 20 years or so it's this. Irish Mums now have the ability to confidently choose how and when they decide to become a parent. Sometimes that initial choice may be made somewhat subconsciously of course but still the plethora of choices and level of control now available is staggering compared to a few short decades ago. Birth plans, vaccinations, community support, religion, schools are now thankfully discussion points instead of a predetermined 'choice' dictated to you. It seems like an obvious point to make until you remember that the term 'Family Planning' didn't really exist during the teenage era of my Mam and her peers. They were somewhat starved of such information and facilities when they were beginning their journey into parenthood. Suffice to say that family planning pretty much began and ended on their wedding day, all that remained was the execution of said plan.

Today thankfully it's entirely accepted and indeed promoted that a couple can now pick and choose when they decide to begin a family be they married or not. They can strategically schedule their career around the time required to dedicate themselves to their children in the early stages before returning to the workforce if the choose to. The fact that these decisions & choices exist for women now just goes to show how far we've come as a society, as a civilisation even. Unfortunately it is light years away from the decisions & choices that my Mam never had the opportunity to even consider over half a century ago. Her choices were made for her by the society she inhabited and in particular the influence of those good old nuns and priests of the Catholic Church...

"Do you think I wanted to have five kids? Or even have a child when I was passed 40 years of age?"

Keep in mind she was saying this *to* the very child she had after she turned 40...

"...We just did what we were told. Our life as it was to us was to get married and rear children. You were given some lessons on natural contraception from the nuns but it didn't really help us understand and you dare not ask any

questions for fear of the cane or worse. If you had a job beforehand you were quickly let go or expected to give it up and the same went for your schooling. Friends & social life were gone too because your husband was working and you were raising children mostly while pregnant with another one. I nearly didn't make it through that time it was really a very dark and scary time for a young woman. Luckily we had the ladies club which I have no doubt kept myself and more than a few others sane and alive during those early years. We got together like we had before we got married but instead of chatting with hope like we used to before, we shared the emotional burden we all carried as a result of the roles that we had been pre-ordained to fulfil. And that's if you were lucky. If you were an unmarried mother it was much worse. But we got each other through it and managed to raise a good family..."

I wish she had stopped reminiscing at that point...

"...But whatever about your brothers & sisters, we certainly didn't expect to be having another child by the time you came along. It nearly broke up our marriage to be honest. But sure we got through it and here you are..."

Eh…Thanks Mam! And they call that a simpler time?? Women of my Mum's generation must look on in disbelief at how standards have changed for their daughters & grand-daughters. But to this day I've never noticed so much as a hint of envy or discontent at how things have improved since their day. In eyes of most parents their kids and grandkids are justly reaping the windfall from the hardships they suffered so the next generation of the family could live better lives in better times.

In a way that sense of noble sacrifice is the very essence of what being a parent is all about. But in return parents get to beat their kids over the head with stories about the scale and nobility of all those sacrifices until their dying day. Turns out there are some perks to being a parent after all. At least we have something to look

forward to in a few years!

_____

Three

Intermittent Communications

" – I'm late..."

" Late? You mean...?"

" Yes I mean... (!)"

"By how long? (*I'm not going to even understand the answer but I have to say something*)"

"Three days (*why are you asking ridiculous questions you don't understand...just listen PLEASE*)..."

"...(*yep I've no idea whether that's good news or bad...what else can I ask...oh f*ckit she's staring at me and I need some time to think so I'm just going for a hug*)..."

"...(*phew, I really need this hug, I love you*)..."

"...(*ok, lets think about this...how f*cked are we?!*)"

- Rob, Dad of Two

The moment you find out that 'you' are pregnant is both an intensely individual and shared experience. No other moment delivers such a blended cocktail of emotional responses from both mothers & fathers to be. Pride & excitement tinged with panic & fear. Stress draped in joy. Outward pouring of reassuring confidence in traffic with an inward flow of internal worry of how unprepared you really are. The only universal constant is that deep down at a truly basic human level, whether you are aware of it or not, you are both feeling the same new burden of responsibility. You are both, now and forever, responsible for the life of another human being. The trouble is how rarely that shared emotional load is actually…well, shared.

Now I'm no new-age hippy when it comes to sharing as it's not always a prerequisite for happiness (just ask a four year old on his birthday). There are loads that can be and should be shared especially during those long (yet in retrospect all too brief) ten months of gestation. Fears & worries, whether they are financial, physical or existential need to be aired or they will fester and erupt amidst an innocuous disagreement over the colour of the baby's first vest. Especially when (God forbid) this momentous news was neither expected nor overtly desired by either or both parties. I don't like the word accident in relation to conception but I do understand why some people apply the term from the outside in. I recall a neighbour's reaction to the news we were expecting our second child...

"Ah jaysus, god luv ye, was it an accident?"

"Eh no, no we planned this one."

"Jaysus ye won't be able to swing a cat in your place will ye"

"....Yeah I guess so...well we better be getting inside now BYEEEEE!"

Some people just know what to say to make you feel all warm inside. Unexpected pregnancies are stressful enough and require a lot of positive constructive thinking on the part of the newly informed parents-to-be. I think it's safe to say that directly asking them 'if it was an accident' will be counterproductive to any of the efforts they are making to cope. Just like at a funeral, sometimes if you don't know what to say the best thing to say is...

"I don't know what to say..."

You can't go too far wrong with that. But accidental or not pregnancy should never be considered a personality defect. If you are enjoying this book so far you will remember the fact that this wonderful talented and utterly humble author was in fact 'an accident'. My mother delivered me into this world herself, single handed on the side of the road in a blizzard during the great depression at the age of 42 and still got home to prepare dinner for the rest of the family. Well, that's how she tells it but one thing that the calendar will confirm is that she was 42 which means after a ten year gap since the birth of my nearest sibling I was most definitely not part of the plan. But an accident, as in not meant to be? I'm not so sure. Should I and everything I have said or done over the last 34 years be dismissed as 'should never have happened anyway...complete accident'?

Besides, statistically everyone on the planet including those who consider me &

other 'unplanned' pregnancies an accident are only here by an unfathomable sequence of happy coincidences too. I won't bore you with the specific figures but in simple terms; the chances of this rock we live on being in an appropriate position to support life are about a billion to one. The fact the life as complex as us sprang out of some prehistoric pond and evolved from single celled organisms into the likes of say, Jedward, is at least another billion to one shot. And finally (without getting into the mechanics of sex) the chances of eggs, sperm, fertilisation and successful cell division all coalescing to form the little person who can subsequently 'go do a wee' by himself are easily in the trillion to one shot category. So in short, Life whether it is formed or desired in a planned manner or completely out of the blue is simply

miraculous and accidental in equal measure.
No one should ever have to fear the tut-
tutting of the village elders in this
context. The creation of life is the
pinnacle of biological & chemical
engineering, ring or no ring.

That's not to say it doesn't scare the
shite out of you!

But that fear needs to be shared or it
could tear you apart. True, there are
certain things which are not necessarily the
most appropriate for common consumption
between partners. Men should be careful in
particular to not volunteer too much support
unless they are of a very stiff
constitution. Listen by all means but push
too far and you could find yourself
discovering new words like 'perineum'. You
could also unfortunately discover new

meanings for words you already know and like. For example if I say the words show & discharge you might visualise a dramatic police thriller about a renegade cop who is discharged due to an excessive show of force. However, in the world in which you are now an active participant, show & discharge mean two awfully different things.

As an expectant father, for example, reading the pregnancy books will garnish you instant brownie points. Guaranteed to instantly diffuse a bad mood your 'birthing partner' may be experiencing at any time. Be careful what you wish for though as some books, and more so anything that happens in a hospital from now on, will irrevocably change your vocabulary & perception regarding the 'beautiful miracle of childbirth'. At least one person from the previous generation will offer to attend all appointments & the delivery itself on your behalf. This offer will most likely offend you and will almost surely be politely rejected by you. You believe this is your role and you are 100% up to the task. Then later there will come a moment over the next few months possibly just before the happiest and most proud moment of your life where you will wish you had simply accepted the offer and gone for a pint instead.

Thankfully you both get a gradual & phased introduction to the world of scans, appointments & stirrups. But once you reach the delivery room all bets are off and anything goes. This is as elemental and awe-inspiring as biology and medicine gets. Even if your plan dictates that Daddy-to-be will stay 'north of the equator' chances are he is still going to see some stuff that they occasionally use to weed out the weaker students from medical school. Nothing can prepare you for it and it will scare the life out of you both but if you can push through your mutual fear-fuelled awkwardness you will encounter a shared experience like no other. But in order to even make it into the delivery room side by side a lot of choppy water must be traversed in the preceding 35 weeks or so.

They say there are seven stages in coming to terms with significant change. Usually around step three you find what is by far the most important realisation when it comes to pregnancy, acceptance. Planned or unplanned, hoped for or dreaded this news is as real as it gets and is going to change both of your lives permanently. The sooner you both accept and make peace with that fact the better the chances are that this change will be for the better, significantly. That is obviously a lot easier said than done however.

As you may have now gathered when the *wonderful* news was broken to us it was a bit of a shock. It wasn't one of those picturesque moments you see in the movies where the lovely charming doctor congratulates a couple each with their hand clasping the others and its smiles all round. No, on this day as Lucy was feeling very ill she began to fear that it might be a little more than a simple tummy bug. But deep down she trembled, hoping that it really wasn't what she began to contemplate it just might be. For my own part, at that very moment, I was driving home from work around noon with an acute case of man-flu that required urgent release from work. My girlfriend might have been feeling physically dreadful and on the receiving end of life changing news but I had a sore throat and a runny nose, easily on a par as any man would testify.

So when my phone rang on the way home and Lucy said she needed to talk to me right away my initial reaction was to be awkward, difficult & selfish. All I was thinking about was a duvet, some DVD's, a Lemsip and my PlayStation. What Lucy was hearing was non-committal horseshit from the man she was now trying to visualise raising a child with.

So she insisted and I relented but so far this was hardly what she needed to hear at that moment. Especially considering her first reaction when the doctor confirmed the pregnancy was to leave the surgery quite abruptly leaving her purse behind in a daze. Naturally as a smoker her next action was to reach for a cigarette to calm her nerves before swearing loudly after realising she couldn't bring herself to light it. Not now with the news that there was a tiny person breathing what ever she took into her lungs with her. The only thing she needed at that point in time was to see me, tell me and I guess see how I would react...after I finished talking about my man flu obviously...

"...I'm ok I don't worry, my nose is blocked and I feel wrecked but I'll soldier on, aches & pains all over but I'll get into bed shortly and sleep it off with some Lemsip and I'll get over it...my throat is very sore too and...hey whats wrong with you your shaking?"

"...........(*continues shivering, tries to speak but nothing comes out*)..."

"Hey, come on tell me, has something happened? Are you ok? You mentioned you were not feeling well, what is it?"

"………(*still unable to say it*)"

"(*ok, I know its NOT this but I'll just ask it to get it out of the way*)…Are you pregnant?"

No words pass her lips but her gaze is locked on my face. I suddenly realise that if it wasn't that…she would have said it by now…

"Come here, it's ok, we'll be fine come here to me…(*hug…HOLY SHITE!)…look at me, we'll be ok, we can do this, ok?"

"………(*sniff, wipes tears away, looks at me)…Ok…(*deep exhale as shivering gradually abates)"

Both our heads were spinning but we did not talk about that. Our thoughts raced through the next few months and years down the paths our lives had now been redirected, now was not the time to debate that. For now we just needed to know that we were in this together. So we hugged, lay on the bed and said little else for the next few hours. A tiny seed of unspoken mutual resolve had sparked into life between us. That was enough for now. Other thoughts unspoken in the months ahead would cause far more damage unfortunately.

Next up though, our minds began to turn towards what was another big step for us, telling our folks. Breaking the unexpected news to them caused more nausea for both of us than the morning sickness already pole-axing Lucy on an hourly basis. Both our mothers are devoutly catholic and can always be found close to the front pew at more than a couple of masses a week. An extra reading that needed saying, lighting a candle or two for the struggling souls of the world they could always be called upon. Now we were about to do the unthinkable. Tell our 'Irish Mammy's' that their respective, unwed son & daughter were going to have a baby. We fretted and panicked about the toll we were about to unload upon them. But there was always our acceptance leading us to hope that maybe, just maybe, they might accept the news with minimal denial and anger too.

There was no point in telling them or anyone else however until we got the news 100% confirmed which meant a return visit to the doctor. Which in turn unfortunately meant waiting a full seven days until the following Monday. Now I've heard people talk about being lost at sea or in the desert and how time seemed to stand still for days on end. And although I'm no castaway or Larry of Arabia I can only sympathise with such people after experiencing that endless week drag on and on. Lucy practically moved in with me for the week. She knew she would crack if her mother noticed how preoccupied she was and probed her as to the root cause, which she no doubt would have. The plan was that we would support each other and stay upbeat in tandem. Nice plan, but to be honest we spent the whole week in zombie mode wishing the days off the calendar and doing our utmost not to let our anxiety spill over into unnecessary, unhelpful arguing.

So after a week without end finally came the doctor's appointment which, once we were there, flashed by in a blur of dates, books and phone numbers. We nodded blankly as the GP scanned our blank faces for signs of panic, distress or fear. She did not have to scan too closely as our faces were drenched in all three. But we were *both* feeling it, together, that much remained solid and true. With that in place there was still hope for our fledgling duo successfully becoming a trio. Next up however was a crucially important factor in that potential success, support from our folks. So we packed our blank expressions into the car and headed for Blackrock, next stop the soon to be 'Nanna & GranDad' Ryan.

Abbey Road in Blackrock might have been just a short five minute drive away but it took almost an hour to get there. That included four minutes to get to the rectangular shaped roundabout at the bottom of their road and the next 45 minutes of Lucy circling said roundabout terrified of the exit that would lead us to her parent's front door. But exit we did...eventually. We exchanged pleasantries and sat down in the kitchen before it became apparent to Lucy's mother that her daughter was about to vomit or faint, possibly both. Panicking she asked what was wrong but Lucy could only stare as the words tried but failed to make it past her lips. I did my best to support her whilst reassuring her folks that I was not about to leave their pregnant daughter to get through this ordeal alone…

"How would you feel about being grandparents?"

I don't know if I sounded as assured as I hoped I had, any more than I know what their instant unspoken reactions were. What I do know is the reaction they showed us and it was unbridled support. We hoped as much but never dared to expect it. Thankfully, instinctively their only thoughts at that moment were for their daughter who was terrified and needed comfort & hope. The mother & daughter hug that followed my announcement was drenched in both. Her Dad didn't know what to say or do any more than I did so we just shook hands which at least told me I was in no danger of being beaten over the head with the Monday sports section of the newspaper. At least not until we were alone. The bottom line was we had told them and they had supported us which made a massive difference to us. I'm sure part of them was just as overwhelmed as we were but they never let it show. After the never-ending week from hell we finally started to feel a little hope and could breathe a little easier. All we had to do now was welcome my own mother out of the knee surgery she had that morning with the news she was going to be a grandmother for the seventh time. Just what her doctor would have ordered.

We were more poised & confident thanks to the support we had received from Lucy's folks so the words flowed more easily. The reaction was almost identical thankfully. My Mam immediately reached for Lucy to reassure and congratulate her in equal measure while my Dad hugged us both briefly to show his support in his own understated fashion.

I have thought in the last few years that both our mothers put their faith in second position compared to their daughter (in-law)'s well-being. Perhaps it's possibly fairer to say that it was their faith in the good parts of being an Irish catholic mother that instantly made their only concern to care for and support their children in a time of great stress. Only they will ever know. Either way that night, for the first time in over a week, we slept. We may have just dropped a bombshell on our folks but they had lifted a huge weight from our shoulders. Our attention began to shift to their new impending grandchild. Now that we had told other human beings it was all the more real to us. Our baby was on its way, due for arrival in 34 weeks or so. We still had no clue exactly how we were going to do it but we needed to get a clue...and fast.

Four

Deliverance

"-Obviously we'll see what happens but I really would like to have a natural birth if possible. I just don't want him or her born all groggy and doped up not knowing where they are. Yeah it will be painful but I really would prefer to do it naturally without the epidural. That way I can be up and about soon after and we're all heading home..."

Two weeks, five hours and seven centimetres dilated later...

"DRUGS! PLEASE GIVE ME SOME PAINKILLERS! Hi Hello? Hello Hi Hi I'm sorry but I really think I need the epidural can you give me the epidural please? Please just give me the epidural"

"Sorry luv, I'm just the tea-lady...I could get you a biscuit? Or how about a-"

*"Oh F*****ck Offfff Someone get this gobsh*te out of here and GET ME SOME DRUGS!*

The wondrous miracle of childbirth is, for the most part, anything but wondrous. Have you ever wondered what your angelic & maternal partner would sound like if she was about to transform into the incredible hulk? Have you ever wanted them to scream into your face while dislocating your fingers as if you were the root of all evil and the reason they are in the most excruciating pain they have ever encountered? Well if so you are in luck, Welcome to the Delivery Room. The room where 99% of your worst fears are realized, the other 1% is the most important life changing moment of your life. The catch is that you have to go through the former to truly experience and appreciate the latter.

For better or worse at least Dads now have the *option* to actually experience and partake in the delivery process. If it's not your thing then you are not the first and won't be the last father who is not present at childbirth. Having experienced it first hand twice now I completely understand why some guys think it's not their place. It's very much an acquired taste to say the least. The strange thing is that, today, Dads who agree or choose not to be there during labour and delivery are very much in the minority. When my eldest sister was born some fifty odd years ago it simply wasn't the done thing. My Dad dropped my Mam and her nightdress to the door of Holles Street hospital at 11 o'clock on a Wednesday evening before heading home again. My sister wasn't born until exactly 24 hours later but in the interim there was nothing expected of my Dad other than to be on hand to bring them home when they were released. But he was ahead of his time so he still tried to help. Well, sort of.

Himself and my late uncle John arrived in on Thursday morning looking uncomfortable but determined to make themselves useful. They asked my Mam, who was by now in no physical or mental state to suffer fools lightly, what they could do to help. My Mam, as the woman she was and still is to this day, had only one use in mind for them. If she couldn't do it herself they were going to do it for her...

"...Pray....Aaaaarrrgggh....Prayers...Go across the road to the church and pray for me and the baby...Prayers...The church...light a candle and say a few prayers pleaseOoooohhhhhh"

The mixture of watching her in pain and the fact it was childbirth meant the two young men needed no encouragement to heed her request and make a sharp exit. They both loved her dearly, one as his wife the other as his older sister. They knew what they had to do. She was in need and she had been clear with her requirements. Prayers, candles and more prayers. They stood on the steps on the hospital, looked over at the church, took a deep breath as they cast a glance at each other and promptly trotted into the nearest pub for a few pints.

I only wish I had known these things about my Dad when I was an unruly teenager. All those times he quizzed me as I arrived home late, chewing five pieces of gum to hide the fact I was stinking of cider. I'd hold my breath whilst trying to sneak past him into

my room thinking all the while thinking he
was an eternal pillar of virtue. He still
pretty much is but these little deviations
from the straight & narrow I keep uncovering
only heighten my admiration for him. And for
my Mam too for putting up with him through
those early years when a lot of her work was
very much done single-handedly. Still
though, picturing the image of him & John
trading church pew for bar-stool in spite of
my Mams devout directions is priceless to
me. As she fought and struggled to bring her
first child into the world the likely lads
stuck there head in again to see if there
was anything they could do. They tried to
look as pious and penitent as possible since
they had apparently spent the previous few
hours in the presence of our Lord. However
they must not have had any of my magic
chewing gum to hand as my Mam knew straight

off from the look and smell of them where they had been. She sent them packing with brutal force so she could focus on finishing her efforts to deliver her child into the world. And she did, after 24 hours of brutal labour she always hastens to add. The following morning herself and my newborn sister woke to the sight of a skulking apologetic young man standing beside them. In his hands a tiny baby-grow suit for his daughter. He didn't even know what a baby-grow was just a few days before. But there he was and thankfully for him my Mam was in too good a mood not to forgive him and introduce him to the newest member of the clan.

But Dad's should always be fore-warned and fully aware. During labour, especially within the confines of the delivery room, comedy or self-interest are generally not well-received. It's an endurance sport mixed with tightrope walking. It only takes one poorly-timed pun or an ill-conceived wink to suffer serious injury or a lifetime of occupancy in the dog house.

It's no doddle for the mother-to-be either. Though to be safe I wouldn't get into comparing the trials & tribulations you both experience, it just won't end well. And to be fair, controversial as this may be to some, there really is no comparison, sorry Dads. What you are about to witness your other half endure and accomplish in producing another human being, like some rabbit *way* too big to be pulled from its magicians hat, is nothing short of jaw-dropping. And the even better news is you can now never again come out on top in any argument on any topic for the rest of your life together. This amazing feat of human engineering & natural instincts is going to be the full stop on every argument you ever have in the future and you cannot argue against it regardless of how unfair you might feel that is...

"- Darling? Did you spend the last of this month's disposable income on a pair of luminous pink high heels you will only wear once?"

"...Emmm, I dunno, did you tear 4 inches of your vagina bringing your offspring in to the world?"

"...............great shoes is all I was saying, very nice on you"

Harsh I know but ultimately fair...in an unfair sort of way. And it's not only the pain & potential injury that mother hens have to contend with. There is also the small matter of dignity. For the previous ten or so plus years women have been, to varying degrees, very proud of the mystique with which the female body is shrouded. If they wear a short skirt they are always very aware of how they sit and the potential view they are exposing other people too. Well, that is apart from over-indulged celebrities clambering out of limousines with as much grace as a dog licking its own arse. Be it in the form of low cut tops or mini-skirts ladies, up until this point, have enjoyed a certain amount of control and allure about who see's how much of their body and when. That all ceases the minute labour begins in earnest. The hospital porter may as well frisk you for your dignity at the front entrance and confiscate it. You won't require it in the delivery room.

From here on, instead of mystique and allure, the women will assume the position and visibility of an open car bonnet. Endlessly quizzed over, prodded and commented on by a dizzying number of faceless people in scrubs. The area of a woman's body that they have been educated since being a toddler to hide & protect is now on display for the world to see. The lady garden has just swung open its gates to visitors and also has some nosey neighbours peering over the side fence for a good gawk. Dignity has left the building. There is some good news though. As difficult as this might be to imagine, at this point in time you will not care in the slightest. The cast of Les Miserable's could file in one at a time to analyse your under carriage while stroking their beards and you won't bat an eyelid. This is due to the fact that around this your biological instinct will take over. Whether you like it or not nature is about to take its most primal of courses. This is what your body was designed for and it knows what to do even if you don't. Whoever the audience may be is irrelevant, you are about to show them just how incredible life in its very purest and raw sense can be. And nothing will ever feel the same again. Including sex. Sorry but it's true, for at least a while anyway. Not in a bad way either, just a little different. And not even necessarily in a physical way but more psychologically. After this night it may take a while before a new Mum feels ready & comfortable with their partner to engage in the act of intimate love-making. Or to put it another way...

"After what I've just been through you are never touching me with __that__ ever again so you may as well tap it on the head with a cold spoon"

Speaking of uncomfortable love-making, remember that giant male nurse who was inserting something into my girlfriend as she was bent over the side of the bed? Well by now you've probably figured out (I hope) that this is not quite a story about 50 Shades of Grey or anything like that. No, colour-wise its more about the deep pale white colour my face turned as said male nurse was administering an epidural to the base of my partner's spine. I actually remember this particular instance with a strange sense of pride. As I've mentioned a lot of what happens inside the delivery room would happen almost identically whether the 'birthing partner' was in the room or not but I really did my best to try and not be that fifth wheel. Or at least not be a fifth wheel that sends the car careering into a roadside ditch. My job was to keep Lucy still and focused on me rather than the enormous needle about to pierce the skin on her lower back. It was just like back on the couch in my front room 9 months earlier. We were out of our depth, scared senseless but somehow we pulled through, together.

As cheesy as it sounds Dads can actually contribute quite a lot if they are interested enough and allowed to. One must be careful what they wish for though. Over-zealous mid-wives could seize on your interest and offer you more, possibly a *lot* more, responsibility than you can handle.

No sooner had I completed my best impression of Rocky Balboa's coach during the epidural process to ensure Lucy stayed focused and didn't budge (which apparently could have crippled her) than I was being asked to insert drips & and reposition colostomy bags. And then came the immortal words of the midwife which I will never forget…

"- Now JP if you just want to grab a leg there and throw it over your shoulder we'll get this baby out together"

Now this was most definitely not part of our 'birth plan'. Our 'birth plan' by the way consisted solely of;

"- Stay by my head, keep a cold facecloth handy and don't make a holy fuckin' show of yourself"

So my promotion to assistant midwife was wholly unexpected by both of us. But again, for both of us, instinct was in full swing by now so I was proud to be asked. And my

wife-to-be? She couldn't have cared less at
this point who was looking at her 'Mary' as
long as the end result was the removal of
the tiny person currently threatening to
fracture her pelvis. And so I grabbed her
left leg, threw it over my right shoulder
and we got to work. Unfortunately despite my
best efforts I cannot begin to describe or
depict a single thing that I saw for the
next half hour or so. For some reason when I
do try to recall everything I saw during
that time I am reminded of the first 15
minutes of 'Saving Private Ryan'. Maybe it's
for the best that my memory of that chunk of
time is particularly hazy.

As a thirty-four year old man who was
about to become a father I was not
completely unfamiliar with the female form.
However at 45 minutes past midnight on the

2nd of May 2009 I could have sworn I was
looking at a difference species entirely.
You have no idea what's going in & what's
coming out and I vaguely recall finding a
spot on the wall to focus my gaze on for the
first ten seconds or so even though I was
but centimetres from my partner's almost
fully dilated cervix…or perhaps *because*. I
was terrified and enthralled simultaneously.
And I genuinely do remember thinking that I
was very glad to be in this position.

That strange admission is due to the fact
that over the previous two hours on several
occasions a loud alarm had sounded from one
of the countless medical devices connected
to Lucy. After what would seem like an
eternity each time a nurse would rush in,
examine the endless printout from the loudly
bleeping machine, make a note and then

leave. Only to return a few minutes later

with a tall polished man in an expensive

looking suit, whom we could only assume was

a consultant. We had to assume a lot because

we were being told nothing. Not who he was

or what the machine was monitoring, what the

alarm was trying to alert them of or

basically what the hell was wrong with the

baby and its mother. I'll never forget

trying to keep Lucy focused and relaxed

about her task as she lay on her side facing

me while over her shoulder I could see a

flustered medical discussion about *something*

coming out of a machine connected to her

abdomen. I had to know what was wrong. Under

the pretence of nipping out to the toilet I

grabbed the nearest recognisable nurse I

could find in the hall and quizzed her about

what was happening. I was hideously out of

my depth in that conversation and understood little of what she said other than;

"- ...is fine but...taking too long...need to move things along as quickly as possible"

I knew she was dumbing it down for me so I read 'quickly as possible' as 'NOW' so as she walked away to her station I just remember thinking to myself...actually to be honest this was more than a thought, this was a prayer. A literal Hail Mary from someone who needed help from a divine source he had not visited outside of a funeral or wedding in decades. I prayed blindly and asked for my girlfriend & baby to be ok. Whatever else the cost was, my job, my car (both were shite anyway) and everything I could offer in the hope that we could all make it through, that's all I wanted. So when presented with the brutal physicality of impending childbirth just a couple of hours later I was delighted just that everything was still in play so to speak.

And so it was time for us to round the final bend and head for the finish line, pronto. Well, the midwife Carol and Lucy did the vast majority of the running to be fair. I'm still unsure as to what I contributed but I what I did know was that my girlfriend was exhausted, physically & mentally. She just wanted to stop. But unfortunately stopping was only an option after the greatest physical exertion of her entire life to date. I did what I could to encourage her to keep going. I cajoled her like a Hollywood actress playing a mid-wife and hoping to win an Oscar for her earnest inspiring performance. I didn't care how

silly it sounded or looked because it was
pretty much all I could do to help. And I
knew this needed to end quickly so I was
going to give it every ounce of sincerity I
could muster. We needed her to keep going
and breathing and pushing and fighting way
past her own pain threshold, which is light
years beyond mine I might add, it's not even
close. With a leg each myself and Carol
(who's performance was such that if a girl
had arrived into the world her name was
undoubtedly going to be Carol too, she was
simply immense) coaxed Lucy down the home
stretch. Deafening noise, bodily fluids,
sheer panic all built to crescendo until the
most remarkable thing happened. A tiny
little person's head came into view. I
gasped in wonder at the craziness of it. I'd
read the books, seen the documentaries but
here just inches from my face was a tiny

little head face down being brought into the world through sheer force of will. Then I panicked. To myself I whispered... ***"Why can't I hear anything...why is there no crying?"***

Not a decibel. Shoulders still inside, the little head was completely motionless and my heart was racing into my shoes and through the floor beneath them. I didn't let on. Lucy wanted to see but Carol kept us honest and reminded us there was still more to do. With one more gargantuan effort the population of the planet has increased by one...or had it. I have never been more deafened by silence then in that seemingly endless sequence of seconds. And then it came, a muffled fluid drowned wail...but a wail nonetheless. My heart did a U-turn and nearly exploded out of the top of my skull. I could see him but after putting all the work in Lucy was still in the dark given her positioning and was desperately asking if the baby was ok followed by asking if boy or girl. Carol confirmed he was fine but then made her first and only mistake of that long night. She turned to me to make the announcement of what we could clearly see to my wife. Unfortunately I had lost the ability for speech about 23 minutes earlier…

"- So Daddy, do you want to tell Mommy what we have here?"

*"- ……………………………………………………*blank stare*"*

I couldn't string any sequences of noises together that would even remotely sound like words so I was of no use at this point. Carol helped me out by informing Lucy herself that we were now the shocked and awed parents of a baby boy. She further enquired upon the name we had decided on for the baby. We had agreed on the name of a boy months earlier and I knew that name like the back of my hand because I liked it so much. But after what I had just witnessed that night I didn't even know my own name let alone that of my newborn son. Lucy, despite being in physical and mental disarray spoke clearly & calmly without skipping a beat.

"Ben"

There's a reason they usually handle the important stuff.

Five

Three's Company

-*Door Closes*

*" (*gently places the car seat in the centre of the room*)...Wow, look at him..."*

*"(*Sits gently on the side of the chair beside his partner*)...Yeah, he's pretty special, all your work babe, you should be proud"*

"And you, he's your son too. We both should be proud. I can't believe we're home with him just the three of us. I thought we'd never get out of that hospital"

"Yeah its great to be home...so far I don't see what the big deal is, he's fast asleep...this doesn't seem all that diffic-"

-*Muffled cry emanates from the car seat almost instantly escalates to a high pitch scream.*

"OH JESUS WHATS WRONG, WHATS WRONG WITH HIM, TAKE OF HIS BLANKET, OPEN HIS COAT"

"IT WONT OPEN, WHERES THE CLIP ON THESE STRAPS???!WAIT I THINK I CAN PULL HIM OUT THROUGH THE SIDE"

"NOOOO! JUST PICK UP THE SEAT, START THE CAR AND GET ME BACK TO THE HOSPITAL NOW!

-Nicole & Joe, Parents of Two

After the surreal environment of the delivery room the itch to get out of the hospital as soon as possible begins to gnaw away at all three of you. First-time Dads usually don't see the rush in the same way that Moms do. Maybe that's because they are sleeping soundly in a big bed on their own while their new family is surrounded by screaming newborn babies 24 hours a day. But regardless of how eager anyone is to get you all home there is a nagging almost invisible question hovering in the back of both your minds…

"What they hell do we do when we get home?"

It seems to make no sense. You are in a medical facility surrounded by experts in infant care. You have no previous experience being responsible for another life other than the goldfish you once adopted that died after a week due to dirty water. Surely it would be more prudent to simply pitch up a tent or stick a beach towel on one of the hospital beds, No? Before you know your meconium from your colostrum, you are being signed out and ushered towards the exit. It's the obvious conclusion to the journey that began when you arrived at the hospital but it's still an unusual thing to get used to; there are now *three* people in the car on the way home. And one of them is entirely dependent on you for food, emotional support, clothing, everything! Some women might already be used to that situation with their husband but for most it's a completely new and daunting experience.

That thought process was somewhat elongated for us. We waited for what seemed to be an eternity for the consultant to come around and officially release. Once she did we started to pack up. An hour later we were still yet to leave the car-park. The main reason for this was an over-zealous attention to detail regarding our infant sons safety. The main culprit however proved to be, and still is, the bane of my life as a father. It's arguably the most difficult foe that a father will ever face. The baby car-seat.

I had spent several hours the previous week trying to cement the base of it into the back seat of our car. That in itself is a nigh impossible task. You have to force it in and strap it down almost 10% beyond the level of being firmly secured so that it is physically impossible for it to come back out. This usually requires opening the instruction manual only to realise it's a series of non-sequential drawings that make no sense. Next after discarding the instructions come a serious of pushes and pulls accompanied by the type of cursing and swearing that make an old dock-worker blush. But eventually its locked into place as good as you can get it. You relax and feel you have accomplished something meaningful. Then along comes a heavily pregnant lady who tries to dislodge it, senses the slightest hint of movement and decrees that it is not safe to put the baby in. And so begins the process anew and an even greater level of swearing and foul language. And that's just the base. The actual seat part is relatively simple, if only the locking mechanism on the straps had been designed by a human and not some sort of alien evil genius.

So at around 3pm on Sunday 3rd^{d} of May 2009 we set about preparing our fledgling family for the drive home. We deemed it wholly appropriate on this gloriously sunny day to wrap Ben as if he was about to climb Mount Everest. His first vest and sparkling set of new clothes were wrapped in a gleaming white cardigan a friend had knitted a few weeks earlier. Around those we enclosed his all in one coat which in turn was covered in a blanket. The blanket had to be pushed down the side of his body into the back of the car-seat just in case he felt compelled to fly out of the seat like Superman on his way to save the day somewhere. All that remained in the process of securing him tighter than Fort Knox were the straps of the car seat. I had studied, analysed and practiced closing them before but now with a precious life underneath them I seemingly lost the ability to use my hands and fingers in co-ordination with my brain. I didn't know whether there were three, four or five interlocking straps and as for the actually lock itself it may as well have been a Sudoku puzzle because I couldn't figure it out. After many minutes of looking like a sweaty panicking gorilla trying to finish a Rubix cube it was done. He was snug as a bug in a rug…and then some. Another sweaty half hour spent wandering around the hospital trying to get change of twenty euro so we could validate our parking ticket didn't help matters either. But eventually we were all strapped in to the car securely and on the road home. The next conversation between myself and Lucy seemingly set the tone for the subtle differences we would always have with regards to our perspectives on parenting...

"(*calm soothing exhale*)...Wow, everything just feels...I dunno, I'm just looking out the windscreen and I see things differently...(*smiles to himself*)...everything looks brigh-"

"DANGEROUSLY UNSAFE, PLEASE SLOW DOWN THE CAR!"

"sorry (*applies the brake gently*) I was just thinking how optimistic and positive everything feels all of a sudden, the world seems a better place all of a sudden, No?"

"No, all I can see from back here is all the potential danger that could harm him, now PLEASE slow down!"

And so I did. We had a queue of traffic
behind us beeping all the way from Cork
Street to Kiltipper as I crawled over speed
bumps and kept the revs below a level
audible to humans. I'm sure we pissed off a
lot of people trying to get home but I
didn't care. We were both right in our
perspectives but all of a sudden the car I
was driving felt like a tank and every other
car was a potential landmine. It's amazing
how cavalier you can be until you have
something of real value to lose.

We arrived home and had those magic few
minutes of silence with each other. But just
like in every kind of dramatic change you
can go through in life eventually comes the
realisation that by and large the world
continues to spin as it always had. Kettles

need to be boiled, food needs to be eaten
and sleep needs to be had.

The kettle especially gets a lot of use in
those first few weeks. No sooner have you
unpacked the hospital bag before the
doorbell rings, a lot. There are generally
two schools of thought on visitors in the
early days. Just keep opening the door
whilst making bucket loads of tea no-one
ends up drinking, or tell everyone to feck
off until you've at least got your head
around your new living arrangements. The
best solution is probably a healthy mix of
the two. The people outside the family
closest to you who have kids themselves will
offer stay away until you've fully settled.
The immediate circle of family will begin to
queue up outside with placards and get very
disgruntled if they don't get to poke & prod

their new relation within 48 hours. All three of you will probably but on such an extended adrenaline and emotional high that you won't feel jaded by the constant flood of visitors for a while. It's probably best to just enjoy it and keep the tea bags coming. Once they doorbell stops ringing the real work will begin. Just in time for your energy levels to realise you've been burning the candle at both ends and in the middle for about 40 weeks now.

If this was a standard pregnancy or parenting book this would be the part where you get lots of advice and recommendations for how to raise the perfect baby. I am in not position of authority to make such recommendations, in fact as I said at the very beginning I don't believe anyone is. This is your home, your baby and the best advice I can honestly give it to figure it out in your own way. Take some of the help that's offered and listen to advice but always keep your own counsel and make your own decisions. If I could be so bold as to impart one little tip that has probably been the biggest help to us it's these three little words. Solid bedtime routine. As soon as you can begin the process of doing the same things every evening that set the mood and expectation for sleep. For us that was, and still is, bath at 6pm, pyjamas and bottle at 6.30, twenty minutes of In the Night Garden (I'll explain later) and then into bed at 7pm. It doesn't happen overnight and it can be incredibly grinding after a while but they benefit in getting this one thing right is immense. They will always wake up at some stage, there will be tummy bugs and literal teething problems too. But overall once they know what to expect once they hear the bath running it makes a huge difference. The time you buy yourself in the evenings completely enhances your ability to function as a parent, partner and human being, just by being able to relax for a few hours and add a few hours sleep to that later in the night. It won't work for every parent much less every child but if you can pull it off you'll thank me someday.

So for the next couple of years our lives were consumed by Ben's daily routine. In amongst that time we managed to organise and pull off our wedding & honeymoon too but that's a story for another book. There were a few lows and more than a few sleep-deprived unnecessary arguments. All of them were eclipsed by a gallery of unforgettably euphoric moments. The first smile, the first time he grasped something or rolled over to reach it, his first Christmas. Possibly more impactful than all of them was, what I consider, the most remarkable achievement in biological history up until the very day it happened. From conception through pregnancy through to crawling and walking all roads had been leading to the event which we had been longing for. The combination of each of our approaches to parenting and all our gentle encouragement for two years had finally paid off when…he spoke.

Ah those first words. All the achievements & accomplishments of mankind over the last 75,000 years or so; fire, farming, flight, fried cheese, all pale into insignificance when compared to the first fully formed words spoken by your pride & joy. You regale others with the context and setting building up to the triumphant arrival of those first few sequential syllables. In reality you are probably hearing more than is actually being said and there is always a tendency to stretch the significance for your audience a little. Nonetheless it is still a monumental moment for you, even if the gravity of the event is somewhat lost on others.

For the vast majority of parents this feels like a day that will never come. You cringe and rile when other people tell you that their slightly younger child has begun to quote Shakespeare while your own is still conversing using a variety of cat-like noises. We began to get a little concerned just before Ben's second birthday as he was still communicating in a way that would see him fit right in with a family of mountain gorillas. According to all the *experts* he should have been ready for Mastermind by now so *obviously* something was wrong with him. The fact that we were so concerned highlights just how much pressure there is when it comes to comparing your child to others. I don't believe any parent actually wants to do that. Well, apart from the Toddlers & Tiara's brigade but don't get me started on that. Comparison just instinctively comes with the territory you inhabit as a parent…

"Ah he's gorgeous, how old is he?"

"Aw thanks he'll be two next week"

"Two?! He's so steady on his feet, and talking so clearly…and is that…"

"Coffee yes, he finds a nice mocha-latte helps him with his reading after his morning art class"

"Oh…of course yeah gosh they're all the same, that's my little man over there, he was two last month and – CIAN Get that worm out of your mouth and where are your trousers?!"

You can't help yourself. You wonder what you have done wrong or not done right that has resulted in the stunted development of your offspring as you compare them to others of their generation. The truth is that comparison is a waste of time, to be frank. All it serves to do is either (a) make you feel bad because you think other people are doing a better job than you or (b) make you feel bad *for* other people if their parenting journey is looking a lot more harrowing & difficult when compared to your own. In other words it serves no positive purpose but it is still nearly impossible to prevent yourself from doing it. I think mothers take it more to heart than fathers. That is ironic because most Dads if left unattended in a group would eagerly set up a betting pool and race their babies against each other. Just to see whose was the best athlete whilst sparing no shame in openly mocking the losers. But Mums will always question themselves and their performance and I think that's what tends to make them so good at what they do. The downside is that by doubting themselves, through comparison with other people's children, they are only adding unnecessary pressure to everyone, not least the little trouser-less worm eater.

All children develop in different ways & on different schedules and the first words will usually arrive just when you begin to doubt they ever will. Aside from the usual baby noises and gorilla grunts, Ben first spoke two words to us one night just short of his second birthday and almost overnight he became a complete chatterbox. So much so that what tends to happen is you spend nearly two years wishing with all your might that they will speak and usually within the next 12 months you will quietly wish at least once that they would just shut up for a minute! I'd love to say that Ben's first words were a haiku or sonnet. Maybe 'World Peace' or something like that to illustrate how wonderful a job we were doing in raising him. But in reality Ben's first real words were none other than...

"Barn Farm"

The name of a TV show he liked. Did we care? Hell no, this earth-shattering and we were ecstatic. He was standing in front of the telly watching his favourite show about some talking farm animals and as the theme song finished with the words 'Big Barn Farm' he turned to us took out his diddly (soother) and said 'Barn Farm' in the most matter of fact manner you could imagine. His delivery was key, as if it was effortless and to say to us 'are you happy now, there I said it now Relax!'. Parenting purists may scoff at the fact it was a TV reference or that he was standing in front of one at the time but did we care? Not in the slightest, our son spoke and the earth moved. Parenting is rarely pure; in fact it's mostly blind luck as you make it up as you go along. So I would avoid building up the 'event' and especially rushing it because pretty soon you'll be wishing you could turn back the clock to the days before the words arrived. And don't expect something insightful either. Trust me a simply 'book' or 'tree' delivered with a surprised tone & smile is all that is required to leave your jaw dangling and heart soaring. And if you're lucky with your reaction they just might give it another go to get even more kudos...we waited...

'...Barn Farm"

There it was again, it wasn't a fluke! Suddenly all those hours spent on your hands & knees repeating the names of random items or pictures hoping for some kind of response have come to fruition and you were completely unprepared. The chances you happen to have recorded the sound 'live' are slim to nil so you immediately begin probing for an encore. No sooner has your little Einstein announced his verbal dexterity to the world than do you spend countless hours asking for a repeat or even more challenging performance. As you might expect, my Dad is always dead set against the practice of encouraging children to 'performing on cue'

"Leave him be, he'll do it in his own time"

Even though my gut reaction is that my fun has been spoiled I ultimately concede that he is (as always, annoyingly) right. There is zero need to rush them into reciting the alphabet or a nursery rhyme because all you are doing is speeding up the arrival of a day that, once it comes, you will wish you had been just a little more patient.

That day came for us just a few days ago when Ben (3 years, 6 months at the time) informed us that…

"In school, the story was about a Elephant"

This may seem a little inconsequential but to us this was extremely distressing. This was the end of a long infinitely charming road that began precisely when Ben spoke his first word. You see for nearly two years Ben had been pronouncing that particular animal very differently. In fact he also had his own version of 'animal' too. Our conversations used to consist of…

"Look Dad, a Ebeshen"

"That's right Ben, good man. Say it with me…E-L-E-P-H-A-N-T?"

"E-B-E-S-H-E-N"

"Nearly got it, one more? E-.L-E-P-H-A-N-T."

"EBESHAN!"

"Ok, we'll work on that some other time"

"Ebeshen is my favourite Amilow"

"Amilow? Ok, one thing at a time"

But now here he was, out in the world, learning his own way and turning our world upside down with this simple word coming out of his mouth; Elephant. After months of gentle cajoling and correcting his pronunciation we realised that he has about to board the train out of Toddler-town and heading for Childhood...and we were not prepared for that yet. So much so that we actually considered coaching him on the correct pronunciation once more, but this time *away* from Elephant and back to Ebeshen. Thankfully our conscience won out over our melancholy in the end.

I guess the point is not to rush or wish anything to come quicker than it naturally will. Or else before you know it you will end up on a YouTube video that shows secret footage of you teaching your child that a cow says woof and a cat says Moooooo. That was nearly us, shameful.

So as Ben headed further into uncharted territory so did his Mam and Dad. As he explored the unknown now equipped with a growing vocabulary we stared into the same unknown future as every other mortgagee in the country who was formerly known as a 1st time buyer. Amidst all the euphoric moments there was one painful question we couldn't escape asking ourselves every day…

" How the hell are we going to provide for him and any siblings whilst living in this thrown together apartment that's now dripping in negative equity?...And what is negative equity anyway?!"

Six

Living in a Box

"What is the difference between a house and home? A house is where you live life to the full and a home is where your children put you when you get old!"

-Brian, Grand-Dad of Eight

You can see where I get my abysmal jokes from.

Our kids may never know the difference but raising them in a two bed apartment is at times, well...crushing. This is not the forum for the 'why & why not' of property bubbles and recessions and in a way its too late for all that anyway. The reality facing my family & tens of thousands of other Irish families is that, to coin a dreadful phrase, we are where we are. So where exactly are we? Our parents would say pretty well off compared to the surroundings they raised us in but as you know by now I'm not a huge fan of comparisons. Unfortunately comparisons are inevitable, especially when your in your folks for Sunday dinner...

"Your Granny Mahon raised 12 of us in a house the size of your bedroom and on most days there was also the aunts, uncles & cousins in too. Nobody starved, we all had clean knickers and got to school on time"

Jesus, and this was supposedly a *simpler* time? If we tried to get 12 kids plus extended family in our relatively spacious two-bed apartment there would be bedlam of biblical proportions. The Gardai would be here in minutes followed swiftly by a swat team of social workers. But back then it truly was a simpler time in one very important way. Everyone, including those in powerful positions, lived mostly within their means and had realistic dreams. You put some money away, maybe get some on your wedding day too and apply for a mortgage. Investment related products meant your pension and that was it. People thought small and slow and as a result things gradually grew over time. House values increased steadily but no one noticed outside of the occasional golf course bragging match or coffee morning dig at an affluent neighbour. By the time you started considering how much your house was worth you were, hopefully, comfortable financially and almost out of mortgage debt. My point is there was a slow-burning route leading in to the future with, at the very least, a silver lining to encompass any dark clouds along the way. A simpler time indeed.

And what of today? Well the world has raced away and gotten itself into a great big complicated mess. Actually at the most basic level you could argue that things are even simpler now than they were back then. Back when my Dad signed his name to purchase our family home for the princely sum of £1920 some 50 years ago. After all, what could be simpler than forsaking all sanity, reason & morality in the pursuit of wealth? That, above everything else, is the impulse that makes the world go around today. Capitalism was of course alive and well when my own parents were looking for their first home. Commodities have been traded for centuries to the benefit of one party, the detriment of another. However, today we have two critical extra elements hitherto unaccounted for. Speed and Greed. Forget all the financial & economic terminology that are just designed to make the most basic self-serving urges of the human condition sound like quantum physics. When you peel it all back it boils down to *'I want more and I want it now'* and most of us are at least at tiny bit guilty of indulging that impulse over the last few years. But a small few of us are a hell of a lot more guilty than others. It's irrelevant which bank they own or what party they are a member of, the only thing that matters is that we, the majority, are the ones left without a chair now that the music has stopped.

The end result of all that desire to consume & accumulate *stuff* is the speed at which financial transactions take place now. They happen so fast that it gives you a headache just trying to contemplate what a bank is doing with your money that's supposedly lodged in your account throughout the course of a minute, never mind a working day. Greed is where the real trouble starts though; again it's hardly a recently discovered phenomenon. The trouble with greed is that now everything is for sale. Not only that but every element of something that is for sale is also for sale individually. Why sell a 4-course meal with one price when you can blend it into a smoothie and sell it a tablespoon at a time at a lower price but sell a far higher amount of smoothie than actually exists at that time? And why stop there? Why not mix your smoothie with loads of other smoothies and possibly slush puppies until you have no idea what ingredients are in your tablespoon before you sell it? Who cares as long as someone is buying it right? Clear as mud? Yep, me too. But I think the plan is for us not to be able to understand it…if so, job well done!

What I'm getting at is that people's homes, people's very lives, are now the commodities of choice. They are bought at discounted prices, grinded up into paste, repackaged and sold all over the world a hundred times over in the same length of time it has taken you to read this sentence. Everyone gets paid and everybody wins. That is until all of a sudden someone realises the emperor has no clothes (or money to repay his mortgage) and the great gravy train runs off the tracks. And what happens next? All of a sudden you look around at your starter-home, your first rung on the property ladder. It's not suitable in any way to raise a family in and yet it's filling up with your kids and their futures…and soon your heart sinks into your shoes. You have the family you always dreamed you might have one day…but not this way, not here…forever?!

We are where we are indeed just like everyone else. Fortunately kids tend not to accept their parents throwing in the towel. It's just not in their nature, something they could do well to teach us. If you find yourself on your knees, head in hands on the sitting room floor you're guaranteed to have one of them sneak up and blow a raspberry on the small of your back. Or stare into your eyes waiting for you to crack up laughing because they know the game you are playing. They obviously don't understand what's going on but it's now irrelevant. That look they give you or even that raspberry on your back should inject all the resolve you need to remember you do not have the option of giving up. They need you, they idolise you and it's at those moments you truly realise how much you need & idolise them too.

Besides as I mentioned at the beginning of this bit your kids are oblivious to the property boom or global financial meltdown. They could be born into a cardboard box with you and not care, to them its home and always will be. On top of that kids can be incredibly low maintenance, sometimes infuriatingly so. You've just spent €50 and four hours of your life purchasing and assembling a bubble car only to discover that the only thing required for an entire evenings worth of giggles is a tea-towel with a friendly face hidden behind it waiting to pop out and say Boo! Next Christmas the boys are getting a set of pots

& pans, some cutlery and a collection of tea towels. When they get bored of them at least they'll go to good use!

The hardest part of raising kids in an apartment is space. Followed closely in 2nd place by the lack of any semblance of a front or back garden, something you really take for granted until you don't have one to speak of. Trying to squeeze the lives of two adults and two kids into one living space plus two relatively small bedrooms can be a nuisance at best. At worst it can have a serious negative impact on everyone's sanity and general well-being. The niggling irritations are daily occurrences. Like when you come back from a full shopping trip designed to feed everyone for a couple of weeks and then have to play fridge freezer Tetris for an hour trying to wedge everything because the appliance is designed for 'apartment living'. Or the fact that you can't open a press, drawer, cabinet or wardrobe without being accosted by something that has been waiting to leap out since it was crammed into the last square inch of space available...

"-Would you grab the ketchup luv?"

"Sure thing, ketchup ketchup ketchup (*open press door*), oh there goes the salt...followed by half the pack of spaghetti, ah here's the ketchup...and here come the rice crispies all over me F*CK THIS PLACE!"

But that blind rage passes easily enough and the impact is minimal. The most negative potential consequence the lack of space can have is on the practicalities of managing conflict. Disagreements and conflict are an unavoidable part of life and particularly common occurrences in the early years of parenting, married or not. Both of you are sleep deprived, stressed about money and struggling to come to terms with the constant pressure of little people depending on you to nurture their every need. Under such strain on both sides arguments are inevitable from time to time regardless of whether you live in a mansion or a bungalow. But when you pretty much have one room to unload your anxiety in it further complicates matters, adds significant strain and causes further unhealthy escalation. How do you get the last word in and slam a door (obviously the best way to win an argument) when there is no other living space to storm into?

Furthermore how do you get everything off your chest and slam said door without due consideration to the one or two impressionable little minds watching this heated exchange unfold but unable to comprehend it? I'd like to say you simply bite your tongue and calmly wait for a more opportune moment to vent when the kids are in bed. But I cannot preach something I have failed to practice more than once in the past. We are all human beings and if we're all honest, imperfect ones at that. You make mistakes and you learn to deal with the anxiety and strain of pressure parenting a little better in the future. It would be a lot easier to do better in the future if we knew there was some better future to hope for. Will they ever have a garden? Will they inherit my debt? Why did I not choose a career in politics!

That's it, rant over. You have to vent sometimes to stay sane so you can focus your attention back on the here and now and what's really important. You have no other choice but to let the depressing stuff go and do the best you can because all that matters is what you can control. You can certainly control the level of recession-related anxiety that you allow your kids to pick up from you. Their little minds are 95% fully formed in the first five years of life. And as such you owe them the duty of care to ensure that all of that 95% is nothing but good stuff. There's plenty of bad stuff that you won't be able to help them with over the course of the rest of their days but those first 5 years are all on you as you set their course for life. All we can do is make them feel happy and secure. Some days that is a lot easier said than done.

I have to admit that I've let my boys and my wife down in the past. The converging pressures of raising a young family in an unsuitable setting on a shoestring budget have gotten the better of us and we'll always have to regret that fact. But we try harder each day to be better than we were yesterday. To work harder to get us and the boys out of here and into the house they deserve. The irony is if, no *when* we walk in to our first proper house with stairs and a garden (ye no, the little luxuries) and gasp in wonder, the boys will probably make a bee line for the car looking to go home. This may be a shoebox in nuclear family terms but it's *their* shoebox. And we have deep roots here beyond the practical restrictions of negative equity and storage space. So many life-affirming and life-changing memories occurred within these poorly insulated, plaster filled walls. First steps, assembling the cot, seeing the two of them

in bath together for the first time, packing
Ben's school bag. Nothing that will go down
in the history books of human civilisation
but to us they should all have been
accompanied by a full orchestral choir and
string quartet, such was the intense emotion
involved. And it all happened here.

More memories which will last beyond our
lifetimes will be created before we lock the
door for the final time. I guess it's not
the market value or square footage or even
the negative equity status of your property
that matters, especially to your kids. It's
what you do inside those four walls, however
far apart they are, in making it a home that
counts. If a shoebox has to be (we are)
where we are for now we'll make the most of
it. With a bit of luck Ben & Dougie will be
telling their own kids, many years from now,

about how their grandparents raised both of

them in an apartment the size of a sock

drawer. The previous generation always has

the tendency and prerogative to exaggerate,

apparently.

Seven

The Invention of Health & Safety

" - If you fall off that wall and break your legs don't come running to me"

-   Janice, Mum of Two.

If you are a parent reading this there is a very strong chance you remember your childhood very differently to the one you are providing for your own kids. Its arguably one of the most commonly overheard conversations in and around playgrounds today...

"When we were kids we were thrown out the door as soon as the sun came up and told to come back when it was dark. If you came home before then you heard all about it

before being sent back out to the field or wherever you were

hanging out at the time...You wouldn't get away with that

today, sure ye couldn't leave your kids go in this day and

age, it's a different time now..."

As parents ourselves we definitely adhere to the end of that statement. But I still constantly find myself asking the same question...Is it really so different today? In particular is it really so much more hazardous and dangerous for parents to raise their children without fear of injury, disappearance or worse? I would tend to argue that things are not so different today versus 'the good old days'. In fact one could argue that children and parents are better protected and more knowledgeable of potential hazards today than ever before. But try telling that to the parents you see shuffling around playgrounds never more than two feet behind their toddler. I'm one of those shufflers by the way and sometimes I have to laugh at myself for being so over-protective. Why do I do it? Why do we cluck and peck like mother hens cajoling chicks around a hay covered barn? Fear and love I guess is the obvious answer. Fear of losing something you love more than yourself or seeing them come to harm. The irony is a well-meaning parent clabbering half-way up a slide to catch their toddler before pick up too much speed is more likely to cause an injury to someone than prevent it. But I don't blame the mother hens. The fear is a little over the top but it's completely understandable. All you have to do is turn on the large rectangular electrical appliance in the corner of the living room to find out why.

Parents today are grilled 24 hours a day from various sources about how dangerous the world around them is for their children. Television, radio, newspapers, friends, family, everyone seems to have a new danger they need to warn you about. Some of this information is invaluable in doing the right thing for your dependents. The sheer volume and tone of some of the dangers discussed can leave you terrified to leave the home though. The list of terrifying dangers is so endless that most parents feel compelled to keep their children isolated from potential playmates, choosing to accompany them at all times instead. Even within the safety of a playground that has been designed by the same safety technicians that NASA used for the space shuttle. It's not only bumps and bruises we are convinced we need to be wary of either. There's cow's milk, bacteria, toilets, soil, drafts, strangers, puddles, sunlight, television, sweets, keys, money, hot, cold, ham, lollipops and on and on. We take it all in. But bizarrely I would wager that most people reading this sentence keep their biscuits and treats in a high unreachable cupboard whilst the toxic cleaning fluids are kept under the sink at a child's eye-level. Again that includes us, go figure.

Thankfully most parents realize there is a balance between safety and well, lunacy. The world is an undeniably far safer place now than when my siblings and I were born and raised. That's before you even consider the obvious dangers that have been eliminated from child rearing over the last few decades. Advances in medicine have made complications during pregnancy and childbirth a far rarer occurrence than ever before in human history. The risk and potential impact of losing a child is never to far from a caring parents mind however. This accounts for the sometimes over-zealous protectiveness most parents shroud their children in. But the question is how much protection is too much? In other words how come the rate of accidents and acquired health issues involving infants is at an all-time low whilst the *fear* of those accidents or issues occurring has never been higher?!

Take my Dad for example. He breaks out in a cold sweat whenever our two boys come within a country mile of stagnant water. Stagnant in so much as it is not currently falling out of the sky or a tap even if it may have just been doing so minutes beforehand. And he has a point to be fair. Idle water in the garden or in the park usually is a breeding ground for bacteria and could lead to a nasty infection if drank in immense proportions or say perhaps you tried to wash out a cut by bathing it in a dark dank puddle. But when the lads happen to wander into roughly the same post code as stagnant water my Dad, with supervising direction from my Mam, will cordon off the area like a police crime scene. Shutting down the area for a few hours until it can be thoroughly sterilised. Nothing dramatically strange or over-zealous about that you might say. That is until you look back once more through the archway of memory lane to when my father was but a gaunt gangly young boy himself. Approximately 65 years earlier he could be photographed in mid-air having leapt from the south side of the Grand Canal. Head first he would dive into a barely liquid sludge consisting of stagnant water, silt and shopping trolleys. The 'den' for the gang of his pals and him was secretly hidden from adult view, buried under thick bushes on the far bank of the canal. So in order to be part of the gang your rite of passage, your only means of access actually, was to dive in and brave the murky water. You didn't so much swim as dive down with enough momentum to reach the apex of the V-shaped mud banks hidden beneath the surface. If you did then the next step was to pull your feet down and kick off again at a forward angle and rise bravely towards the opposite bank, breaking the surface again but this time a proven, worthy entrant to the hallowed gang hideout.

What happened in the years between such

reckless abandonment as he leapt from that

canal bank to the forensic analysis of

innocuous patches of rain-water is not as

mysterious as I once thought. The most

likely cause is the very same as how I came

to fear the inherent dangers of ground water

encroaching upon my own children. He

inherited it along the way and subsequently

passed it along to me. I would laugh at the

above comparison until my wife reminds me

that I also come out in a rash whenever the

boys get down on their hands & knees and

splash in puddles. I used to do the very

same myself and a lot worse besides. But now

I step in with baby-wipes and disinfectant

at the ready. I don't know exactly when it

happened but somewhere along the line my Mam

and Dad put the fear of God in me about

'dirty' water and some years later I peddle

the very same line to my own boys. So I guess at least it's not *all* the television's fault. We inherit a certain amount of caution as we learn to love something we dare not lose or see come to harm. And our parents did the very same. The slightly worrying thing is that some people are force-fed so much fear that they go a little to far in attempting to keep their children safe from harm. Just ask Edward Jenner.

Well that would be difficult considering he's been suffering from a mild case of death for a couple of hundred years. Indulge me in a little side story for a moment. One that illustrates the most bizarre interpretation of protection that I have come across recently, one that would make Mr. Jenner spin in his relatively understated grave. I say relatively because how can you sufficiently reward enough acclaim to a man who has saved more lives than any other person in history? I'm no history professor, I was barely what you would call an average academic student but there's a reason Lucy call's me a nerd and that's because...well, I am one. I like reading books or watching programmes about the big ideas and events that have shaped the world today. Not in a way that I could get a degree in anything particularly fancy but it does make me a bit of a demon at a table quiz! Anyway, back to one such event in the year 1796 and in particular a Mr. Edward Jenner. After literally being spoon-fed a nasty dose of Smallpox as a child (in an ill-fated attempt to cure the disease) the young Englishman decided to become a doctor and to one day ensure no-one else would have to die from the usually fatal disease.

A fine doctor he became and he never lost the desire to rid the world of Smallpox. With the help of some buxom milkmaids, who seemed invulnerable to smallpox thanks to spending so much time around cattle, he realised the eureka moment had arrived. Jenner decided to risk infecting a young boy with a milder disease, Cowpox, on the basis that it would ultimately provide immunity from the more lethal Smallpox. The moment of truth arrived slowly over the next few weeks as Jenner took the crucial step of infecting the young boy with Smallpox itself. Low and behold the boy never showed any signs or symptoms of the disease that had by then already killed millions of people around the world. But that was about to change. Within months Jenner's vaccination (which he named from vacca for cow) was circling the globe, being reproduced and before long death from Smallpox was all but eliminated, everywhere.

Now I'm sure not everyone, especially the young boy, was thrilled about the idea of being intentionally infected with a mild dose of a disease even if it meant saving his life. But it works and it has continued to work for many more diseases ever since. Minimal risk for maxiMum reward you could say. Which makes me all the more incredulous when I listen to some parents talk about their decision *not* to vaccinate their child against anything. This is most commonly because of fear and revulsion regarding the idea of injecting a disease, however mild a dose, into their child. I get it, I really do. I understand the

instinctive drive to protect your son or
daughter from contact within any form of
disease. But when that protection is so
short-sighted that it spares slight
discomfort today at the cost of heightening
the risk of serious complications tomorrow I
really do end up scratching my head. The
first day the child walks in to a crowded
classroom he is going to come home with all
sorts of ailments that have minimal impact
on those around him. Everyone is obviously
entitled to their own stance on every issue
but in this one instance I have to play the
Nike card, Just Do It!

The paranoia we all suffer regarding
disease goes beyond inoculation too. We are
blitzed with advertisements telling us the
dangers of bacteria in the home, the park,
the playground. All you can do to stop short

of a Howard Hughes impression is to run around disinfecting everything & everyone, especially the kids. Sometimes your child enters a playground with a slight runny nose, coughs without covering their mouth and next thing you know there is a stampede in all directions away from them. Complete with parents throwing glares over their shoulder at your cheek for bring *the unclean* into their midst. As with fear of inoculation, I get it. There are few more undesirable tasks as a parent than wiping your kid's nose as they are coughing point blank into your face. So when it's someone else's child the automatic reaction is repulsion and to protect your own. But here's the thing; kids are supposed to get sick, they actually need to. Unless you expect your child to live their entire life like the boy in the bubble they are going to come into contact with viruses & bacteria sooner or later. Inoculation and early exposure is like a coaching session for their body to learn how to defend themselves without going overboard. If you have kept them isolated and 'safe' from all infection until they walk in the door of their sweet 16th birthday party with 200 guests, well congratulations that's a parenting fail. They will be in hospital by the end of the night feeling a million times worse than if you had just let them get a simple jab 15 years earlier.

Perhaps the most obvious example nowadays is Chicken Pox. It's an unpleasant dose to be hit by at any age but the scale of severity dramatically increases with age. A couple of years ago I awoke in the middle of the night feeling like I had been dropped from a chopper into the middle of the Atlantic. As I shuffled around the bed shivering I felt an odd lump on my torso. A worrying blister which triggered a call to my Mam...

"Hi it's me, listen did I ever have the chicken pox as a child"?

"...Oh Jesus I don't know...I remember one of you did but I can't for the life of me remember which one...is that any help to you?"

She can't be expected to remember everything I guess, occupational hazard of an overworked mother to be fair. But now, due to being one of her five children, I basically only had a 20% chance of having a benign though nasty blister on my chest. The odds were against me and unfortunately were proved correct. Within 24 hours I descended

into a feverish, hallucinatory &
debilitating stupor which lasted nearly a
month. The blisters popped up over every
inch of me; hair, face, body (yes *body*),
legs and feet it was diabolical. It took
another couple of months to fully recover
from. I have never felt as awful in my
entire life.

I'll spare you the gory details because
the important thing to note is that about a
week into my dose the boys started to show
signs of having contracted the disease from
me. This served as some relief (though I was
a little jealous too) to see the boys suffer
from just a few spots, a slight drop in form
and come out the other side of it in less
than five days. And that was that. They will
never have to suffer the woeful time that I
did because they dealt with a few brief

blisters which they will barely even remember in a few years. Having experienced the adult version of the chicken pox my advice is if you see a child with a confirmed case of the disease immediately run over and smear your kid all over them. They will thank you for it in later life. Oh but for the love of God verify that you yourself have already had it as a child. Hopefully your mother will have a better recollection than mine did.

Once you have disease covered its pretty much plain sailing in terms of childhood safety. Well, not quite. There are also the myriad of warnings that only become apparent once you bring your child home for the first time. And then a whole new set of dangers present themselves once they become upwardly mobile. We were given a DVD by the local health nurse to prepare and coach us on dealing with infant health & safety issue around the household such as choking, broken bones and drinking bleach. After approximately seven minutes of terrifyingly recreated animations of household accidents the DVD was ejected ahead of schedule and buried in the communal garden area out front. Legend has it that if you finish watching the entire programme your mobile rings and someone in a creepy voice calls you a negligent parent for not wrapping your child in bubble-wrap as soon as they left the womb.

I don't mean to be flippant about accidents at all. We do take a lot of care to ensure obvious hazards are not within reach, that's just common sense. But kids will always find a way of trying or doing

something that is even more dangerous than
what you were originally worrying about. We
became even more aware of that with Dougie
who, when compared to Ben, is a little
bit…violently unpredictable shall we say. We
originally marvelled at how active Dougie
was at such a young age. He was walking from
seven months, which was impressive and
terrifying in equal measure. But soon we
started to see danger everywhere. He was
climbing furniture and opening presses
before we knew it so we had to be almost
military in our dedication to ensuring
chairs were out of reach, presses were
locked and all possible hazards in the room
were cushioned against him having a serious
fall. The DVD would have been proud of us.
But Dougie is an *active child* and they
almost seem to get a great thrill out of
upsetting the planned order of things. So

what does he do one day at the age of 1 and a half? He watches us go through the weekly routine of storing all the hazardous materials away, applying soft corners to all the furniture, deleting all the scary bits from his favourite Disney movies. Noticing that we are distracted by the challenge of protecting his health & safety, he quietly pushes open the front-room window and promptly jumps out of it head first. He was fine don't panic. It was the ground floor and we caught him on the first bounce. The bump was treated with 200 cc's of ice cream and was forgotten just as quickly as it had happened. We'll always have to live in fear of such events with Dougie because he is just a whirlwind of adventurous energy. That's the polite way to put it.

Even the most shy and retiring child will take their share of bumps, bruises & burns. And while that will result in panic and sometimes an unnecessary rush to the emergency room it's nothing to worry about. Just like the earlier diseases, these are milestones of childhood and they are supposed to happen. How else do they learn what they can and cannot touch or what height is safe to climb to? How can they find out how good their balance is if not by trial and error? It's best and almost natural to test out these theories at a time when your body is more capable of healing itself than at any other time in its life. We all need to do it at some stage. You climb, you fall, you get hurt, you learn, you don't try it again…for a while anyway. A sensible balance is attainable between throwing your child head first into a frothy body of stagnant water and never letting a doctors needle come into contact with them. What is required is a little trust in them and usually a lot of wincing from you.

To this very day my Dad still manages to shock me with his varying approaches to health & safety depending on what age he is. Last week we went to Dublin Zoo with my folks. As usual my Mam & Dad are telling us to be careful and keep the boys safe from all the dangerous animals (dangerously sleeping behind 3 feet of reinforced glass)...

"Not so close to that railing...Is he ok on that slide? Is he too warm in that coat, I better take it off...the other lad has no coat, c'mere to Granny and I'll put one on."

...and so on. They are just showing that they care and we get that. Then my Dad begins to tell us the story of his first few visits to Dublin Zoo…

"- They've really done a great job on the place, very impressive how the place has developed since me & your uncle Pat first came here… must be 60 years ago now… Myself, uncle pat and a few of the lads from the road used to walk down to the phoenix park from Galtymore Road and we'd jump the fence into the zoo…"

" Wait, What?! How did you know whether you were jumping into a picnic area or the lion's cage?"

"We didn't really, I didn't matter because we tended not to be there for too long anyway…security always chased us down and turfed us out…"

My Dad as I have always known him can always be found wearing ironed slacks, shirt, tie & pullover, even on a casual Saturday afternoon. So the image of him and his brother being caught by the scruff of the necks by security and flung out of the zoo is fantastic. One minute his face is sparkling as he tells us every detail of how they hopped the fence into any one of the wild carnivore enclosures without a care in the world. The next minute he is panicking at the sight of Dougie leaning to close to a ground level railing. It's funny how our perception of what level of risk is acceptable changes with age. It's okay though. He still gets that twinkle in his eye when he is recalling tales of mischief from his youth so I don't mind listening to him worry and fuss at the sight of Dougie eating a snail or a wasp. Although to be fair we all wet our knickers when Dougie ate that wasp. We must show him that health & safety DVD. I doubt that particular hazard is covered by it.

Maybe we go too far in our efforts to protect them sometimes. Is there any chance they won't resent us for it in the future if we tell them it's for their own good? I doubt it. It didn't work on me apparently…

———————————

Eight

If You Stop Running I Won't Hit You

" - My Mam used to burst all our footballs with the kitchen knife cos we used to belt the ball against the kitchen window. When we down-sized to tennis balls, using the legs of garden chairs as goals, she also downsized to bursting the tennis balls with a smaller steak knife. There are still sports ball cadavers all over the house and garden. Don't get me started on wooden spoons. She must have broken dozen's of them over my brothers' arse and mine"

-   Aidan, Kid

'Do what you're told'. We've all heard it. Some have probably already spoken those infamous words themselves. Sometimes they are not even spoken aloud but communicated to via a stern glance over the rim of a pair of glasses. Either way I doubt anyone has ever willingly conceded that they were happy to do whatever was being asked of them. It's usually not the most preferable option.

Since the dawn of time whether it was a royal decree, government legislation or a scolding from your parents nobody likes being told what to do. But as kids the fact is we *usually* do not know as much as our parents do and sometimes, unfortunately for them that means they have to be the bad guy. It's something we'll never understand until we have to become that very same bad guy ourselves in later life.

One of the most vivid negative memories I remember from my childhood often still creeps into my nightmares. I can visualise it quite easily if I happen to have had too much cheese late in the evening. I am watching the memory play out things through my own eyes as an 8 year old boy as I look up from an armchair in the corner of my Mam and Dads house. I barely fill a quarter of the chair with my tiny body. As my eyes focus I begin to see that my peripheral vision is filled with the faces of my siblings and father looking down upon me. Positioned centrally, my mother is reaching her hands towards me. It does have the appearance and feel of a somewhat positive memory. However if you were to turn up the volume and hear what is going on it begins to take on a different energy entirely. Particularly as I hear my Dad shouting...

"DO WHAT YOU'RE TOLD OR I'LL BOX YOUR EARS!"

My Mam is panicking as she fumbles with a spoon and something else is her shaking hands. My siblings and my Dad are shouting at me and each other as they struggle to

physically restrain me, holding me tightly
down in the armchair. For my part, I am
screaming like a banshee and willing to lose
several limbs if it meant escaping out of
the chair as soon as possible. And then the
source of all the distress and commotion
floats menacingly into view. A tablespoon
shivers in my mother's right hand as she is
creeping towards me. I can't get away from
it this time. Medicine.

They had learnt their lesson the last time
when I nearly choked myself. I forced a gag
reflex as they tried to cajole me into
swallowing the capsule whole. This time the
capsule had been opened and the white grainy
powder swirled in a spoon with some milk.
And now its inches from my immovable head.
My screaming escalates as I kick and twist
to break loose but there is no escape from

it. I try to lock my jaw shut and purse my lips but to no avail. In she puts it, my Dad holds nose until I swallow, I dry wretch but it's too late its down and staying down. Eight minutes later I'm playing happily with my toys while the family relaxes watching telly together. It's like it never happened. But if it had not happened I could have been a very sick little boy as I was suffering from an acute bacterial infection of my respiratory system. I can't be any more specific than that because my Mam doesn't actually remember the exact illness. She has no problem recalling how much trouble I gave her as a patient though. The medicine proved invaluable in helping my body fight back against the infection and I recovered soon after. What everyone mostly remembers is the unholy show I made of myself due to my apparent aversion to medicine. Upon reflection I can't honestly say whether my aversion was due to the anti-biotic itself or the fact that it was being forced upon me against my will. Having found myself on the other side of that dynamic recently with my own kids I am inclined to think it was more a case of the latter.

Today, not only do I understand why they had to force their will upon me for my own good but I also sympathise endlessly with the headache-inducing hassle I caused them. Especially when I find myself restraining a violently bucking child of my own who's running a temperature of 39.8 Celsius and is in desperate need of medicine…whether he likes it or not. The situation from my nightmares almost duplicates itself except for the fact that Lucy and I are grossly under-staffed. One of us needs to administer the drugs whilst the other needs to restrain the furiously flailing limbs. Its only five little millilitres of syrup we need to shoot at the back of his mouth. It usually takes another 25 mils being spat back out or ending up in his hair as he struggles. He hates it. WE hate it. But if his temperature hits 40 he risks going into convulsions and possibly a coma to follow. Then the immortal words fire out of my mouth before I realise I've even lost my cool…

"DO WHAT YOU'RE TOLD AND TAKE YOUR MEDICINE!"

Medical issues are pretty black & white which helps alleviate most of the guilt incurred from forcing your will on your kids. General safety and morality are far more ambiguous. They also have the added complication of highlighting not only the difference in opinion between parents &

child but also between the parents themselves. In general terms nowadays those differing opinions tend to sit at two separate ends of the discipline spectrum. Brute force versus structured diplomacy...

"GET DOWN OFF THAT TABLE NOW!"

"DON'T shout at him, you need to go down to his level...Conor sweetheart, listen to Mommy, come down from the table please or you'll have to go on the naughty chair...this is your warning now sweetheart c'mon"

"THAT'S NOT GOING TO WORK! CONOR, I SAID GET DOWN OFF THAT TABLE RIGHT NOW BEFORE YOU FALL AND HURT YOURSELF! I'M WARNING YOU, I'LL SMACK YOUR BUM!"

"DON'T raise your voice to him, I'm handling it...Conor, you've had your warning now you will go on the chair if you don't get down sweetheart"

"DON'T CORRECT ME, CORRECT HIM! HE'S LAUGHIN AT US AND IS GOING TO SERIOUSLY HURT HIMSELF IF HE FALLS...THAT'S IT COME HERE, YOU'RE GOING IN THE CHAIR RIGHT NOW MISTER"

"you can't just lift and throw him into the chair that way; you need to explain to him and tell him how long he will be there for. Time it exactly and then explain it to him again"

"EXPLAIN? OK, SIT IN THAT CHAIR AND DON'T MOVE UNTIL I SAY SO!...how's that?"

*"good job, well done but you need to be a little mo-
....wait, where are you going?"*

"The pub, the match, remember?"

*"What about Conor, you need to finish the
process...where'd he go?"*

"...AH JAYSUS GET BACK DOWN OFF THAT TABLE NOW!"

"I told you, don't shout at him, you need to-"

*"-forget it, I'm done, you handle it! Leave him on the
table for all I care, I'm outta here!"*

Who is correct? The answer usually depends
on which technique you tend to employ
yourself. The truth is probably a little of
both are correct, the key as always is
balance. It highlights one of the most
frustrating impossibilities of marriage and
parenting. That is when it comes to slight
differences of opinion or heated arguments
no one ever actually wins, someone just
gives up and concedes earlier than the
other. There is a huge amount of money to be
made for someone to position themselves as a

marriage & parenting referee, not counsellor but referee. Imagine how simple it would be to have someone in a black & white striped shirt burst in the door ten minutes into an argument over how best to discipline a child and announce that...

"Based on the objective evidence of the situation the clear winner here is Mom with her 'if you don't come in, the man will take you away' approach. Dad you may now issue your sincere apology and begin your five minute sulking in the bedroom watching Sky Sports News. I'll be back at 4.30pm to announce the winner of Force feeding vs. Just give her one of those chocolate biscuits she asked for in a cute voice"

I would pay significant fees for that service, even if he would probably issue yellow cards for gloating and an on the spot fine for 'I told you so!'

In reality things are never decided in that clear-cut a fashion. So many arguments erupt when it comes to disciplinary measures despite the fact you ultimately want the same thing, to protect your child from harm and raise them to be good people.

Enforcing discipline thankfully has some funny consequences as well as the necessary ones. They include the production some of the most memorable quotes you never ever thought you would here yourself say. Including the gross...

"Stop picking your nose and rubbing it in your sister"

Or the threat you have no way of enacting whilst driving...

"Put your arms back in your straps or I'll put you in the boot until we get home"

To the slightly terrifying...

"If you don't come here right now, the man in the bushes will get you!"

To the downright lying involving innocent bystanders...

'No, the ice-cream man said you were not allowed to get ice-cream because you threw a shoe at the dog' '

It can actually be a lot of fun sometimes, not for the parent trying to dole out the discipline obviously. There are two key motivations driving the desperate need to enforce discipline on your child in a public place. Firstly the honourable desire to ensure they grow up to be good upstanding pillars of the community around them, clearly knowing the difference between right and wrong. Secondly and a little less honourable is the realisation that the actions of your child reflect directly upon your own character in the eyes of those judgemental faces around the playground. Even if that statement is not remotely true, it certainly always feels that way. You can hear what they are thinking as you haul your child to his feet in mid-tantrum...

"-tut- would you look at that, what kind of a mother must she be to let her child act like that? Disgraceful behaviour, I'm sure that brat didn't lick it off the stones either..."

What I love about being in that situation is being comfortable enough to admit I am doing my best to control my child's behaviour and failing. In addition, I look at the most judgemental set eyes fixed upon me and see that they are so focused on my 'failings' that they have not looked at their own child since they arrived in the playground. Meanwhile the apple of their eye is terrorising kids half their size without an ounce of supervision to worry about. Bottom line is, at least I'm trying. I might have zero chance of leaving this playground with an ounce of dignity much less a quiet smiling child. But I'm not too proud to make a complete arse of myself in my vain attempt to show them their behaviour is unacceptable.

At the end of the day people will always judge you especially as you flap about in unwinnable situations in the middle of a public place. Your child's upbringing and long term development is not their responsibility though, it's all yours. So feck them, let them laugh or roll their eyes as your child flops to the ground and kicks wildly at the prospect of having to go home. All you can do is what you believe is right and that's all that counts. The reality is if they were honest those parents, all parents in fact, would secretly sympathise with you because it is something every child will try out in public just to push your buttons. It's our job to se the boundaries and hope the get what we are trying to do for them in the long term.

That's a difficult enough task on its own. It becomes an almost impossible one when you are in need of dishing out some discipline while in the company of a grandparent. It's nearly not worth trying...

"Max! Get OFF your sister and put down that saucepan"

"Ah leave him alone, sure he's only playin, ye aul cod are'nt ye only playin with your sister"

"Please Mam let me handle this...Max, Come Here to Mommy Now!"

"Ah yeah sure do it your own way, what do I know, I only raised six of you"

"Don't start that please Mam, I'm just tryin to- Max! OFF your sister NOW!"

Max senses his opening. Even at the tender age of three he knows how to play the game. The crying starts, no tears mind you but lots of noise and apparent sadness…

"Ah what has she done to ye come here to your granny and tell me whats wrong"

"MAM please he is not getting away with this, let me speak to him and for god's sake don't give him a bisc-"

"Now, there you go my little angel, granny give you a chocolate biscuit to make it all better, there you go now, back out to play with your sister…"

Within sixty seconds Max's sister obviously arrives with a saucepan related injury and a request for chocolate cookies like her naughty brother received for his misbehaviour. As she skips back out to play she leaves behind a smiling grandmother and her own mother with head in hands wondering why she even bothered trying.

If managing a tantrum in public is a no-win situation, trying to manage it whilst fending off the intervention of over-attentive grandparents is just a ridiculous waste of energy. I don't really remember my grandparents as they were passed away before I was old enough to appreciate and understand who they were. As a result, difficult as it is, we try to let the boys have the type of relationship with their grandparents that I never got the chance to, a fun one. Let your folks plough them with cookies, ice cream and watch them behave just as you would expect an over-sugared toddler to behave. That's what kids should feel about a trip to, or visit from, their grandparents, like it's a treat. We can get back to worrying about the long term discipline stuff once the dust settles at the end of a fun-filled day.

You need a regular break from relentlessly trying to impress your own version of the Ten Commandments on your children. Do this, don't do that, put that down, don't eat that, stop biting that cat, where did you get that goldfish from, it really is difficult to keep correcting them day after day. There must be another way or at least a little something to help grease the wheels of the disciplinary process. After all it can't be all stick and no carrot can it? How much does a carrot cost

these days anyway? Can't be that much
surely...

Nine

To Infinite Expense...And Beyond!

"He gets too much stuff if you ask me. In my day we were given a stick of butter, a lump of coal and we were happy to get it. On my birthday the only present I got was a new hat so and my mother made me stand by the window so it looked like I had been given a whole set of new clothes. I was naked from the neck down but the neighbours didn't know it and that's all that mattered"

Chris, Dad of Three

(Doing an exaggerated impression of how his Dad refers to his children)

I never tire of being told about how little a child received by ways of treats or rewards back in the good old days. It's not actually as though they received nothing but it seems sometimes as though the treats I were almost intentionally shoddy just to reinforce the idea that life was so difficult. They also provide lots of ammunition from grandparents to chastise their own children regarding how much they spoil their grandchildren. That's more than a little unfair in this day and age I think. If both parents are working nowadays what's the harm in providing a little jolt of excitement and reward when they eventually get to see their kids at the end of the day? Alternatively if both parents are out of work they need to be allowed the prerogative to round up a few coins and pick even a cheap toy or a happy meal. Even if it's just to reassure both parent and child that they do not have to completely forego the occasional treat even though times are tough. Sometimes it's a reward. Other times it's a handy incentive for good behaviour.

That always tops the effectiveness of punishment being enforced as a result of bad behaviour. I believe the ideas and base motivations regarding treats and rewards have changed very little over the course of human history, much less the last few decades. What has changed is the bewildering array of options thrust before the impressionable eyes of children and subsequently into the wallets of bemused parents.

Toys for example have changed a lot even from my day…did I just say that? Now I *really* feel old. A couple of decades ago all a boy needed was anything that came in a box marked with the inimitable Star Wars logo. I was the happiest boy on the road the day I unwrapped my Millennium Falcon. For a few days at least I was the centre of excited attention with my friends. Sure enough, it wasn't long before long one of them showed up with one of the other big items from the Star Wars range complete with Darth Vader action figure. My day in the soon came to an abrupt end. The next big thing that consumed my attention was Transformers and the exact same dynamic returned. I had the best one and everyone flocked to my house. The following week word spread that one of the other lads had an even better one and my swanky transformer toy quickly ended up as a forgotten yet colourful door-stop holding open the garage door on windy days. I guess toys might have changed in the twenty odd years from those days to this one. However, kids themselves have actually changed very little in this regard. They share that same short attention span and competitive streak to show off the best toys that their parents once did. What they also share with their elders is the lack of willingness to share their toys too...

"Noooooo, I was playing with that car. He took it! I HAD IT FIRST!!"

"Liam stop it, your brother just wants to play with you, let him have that one"

"BUT I WAS PLAYIN WITH THAT ONE!"

"You have all the other ones let him play with that one car, please don't upset him he's only a baby, that's it good man, are you giving him another one?"

"....Alex? here do you want to play with this instead? Here take this toy..."

"Liam that's a spoon, don't be mean to your brother...Wow Alex what did you get, a spoon? Wow that's awesome (*Alex smiles, delighted with his new 'toy'*)"

What happens next is inevitable as the older brother see's what he is missing...

"I WANT THE SPOON! I HAD IT FIRST!"

"Oh for Christ's Sake Liam!!!"

Homer Simpson once announced in celebratory fashion that alcohol was 'the cause of and solution to all of life's problems'. Having refereed multiple wrestling matches between toddlers, over toys that neither of them wanted just a few minutes earlier, I would have to put toys in the same lofty category.

Our eldest sons' first big toy was, like a lot of other boys of his generation, a Buzz Lightyear action figure. It still comes out of the toy box every other day as it still has a place in his heart. What old Buzz no longer has is a head. That's because Dougie arrived and loved Buzz just as much as his older brother did. So a daily struggle ensued which one day saw the dashing Space Ranger fly across the room and take some heavy damage. A lot of ice cream was administered that day to ease the communal suffering. One of the convenient things about having two boys is the fact that the kind of toys one boy likes will most likely make the other happy too. We would always like to encourage Dougie to find his own preferences rather than forcing him to settle for hand-me-down toys but having two boys certainly help reduce cost as well. If we found ourselves with a house full of boy's toys and one day became the parents of a beautiful little princess we'd be screwed for space and money. Thankfully Dougie has been happy to get on board with whatever Ben has enjoyed playing with. Sometimes he has proved a little too happy and particularly enjoys grabbing whatever Ben is engrossed in and running away like a giddy bank- robber, just for the thrill of the chase.

His first toy that was uniquely for him and not something he got into by association with Ben was a collection of plush stuffed characters from In The Night Garden, a TV show I will come back to shortly. He was so used to accepting/grabbing Ben's toys that he was truly humbled to receive something for himself. Five minutes later however he was back in a tussle with Ben as they both fought over Buzz again, regardless of his unfortunate decapitation. Dougie just loves punching above his weight. His sense of wonder at receiving something that he understood as being solely for him was wonderful. It's that sensation which makes toys far more than expensive, dispensable pieces of plastic. For parents and the joyful recipients

I remember that sensation like it was yesterday upon seeing that Star Wars logo peek through a small tear in the shiny wrapping paper many Christmas's ago. For Lucy her earliest memory is of a burgundy coloured corduroy pram complete with a deluxe baby to care for. For my brothers & sisters a couple of decades earlier the biggest events involving toys revolve around bikes & prams respectively. Even further back down memory lane my Mam still beams when she describes how, at aged seven, herself and her sister Lily paraded down the Crumlin road each with their own gleaming miniature Silvercross pram like they were royal nannies. In his own stoic manner my Dad recounts with child-like wonder the frost-bitten morning seventy years ago when a Meccano set was presented to him by the man who was teaching him to play the church organ, Mr Lowe.

It was the stuff of legend. So much so that his friends (and family) were convinced he had stolen it. Once they conceded theft was not likely the rumour then spread that the Morgan's of Galtymore Road had 'won the sweeps' which I'm reliably informed is something akin to winning the lotto today. For a few years that Mecanno set could not be surpassed in the records of unbeatable presents around the community. That is until one morning a very simple spherical object appeared under the Christmas tree. Nothing more than hot air wrapped in pig skin. No not a politician but a football. Well it qualifies as a football considering it had a rubber bladder and was encased in (extremely tough) leather. Footballers of today would probably consider this thing a medicine ball. But to my Dad this was a ball of solid gold. He recalls it actually felt like that to kick it on a wet day too. That mattered little though. Twenty minutes later my Dad plus 35 others boys and girls from the road were immersed in an eight hour long world cup final in the field behind their row of houses. No records of winners or losers exist on public record but many observers have confirmed all participants were in bed unconscious within minutes of Christmas supper being inhaled like it was a stray dog's first meal in a week. A simple sphere of hot air wrapped in rubber and tough leather (now further encased in cold hardened mud) nestled inside the front door. Now forevermore associated with legendary tales recalling the near miss, the wonder goal, the solo dribble and the injustice of that unnoticed foul leading to the last minute winning goal. My Dad and his brothers were immediate celebrities known up and down the road as 'the lads with the size 4 football'.

The magic of toys goes beyond a subsequent increase in social standing. In many ways the magic of toys is as much about freezing a time between parents and child when true innocence & wonder saturates their relationship. Like the time my parents pushed the boat out for their second born son in somewhat operatic circumstances some 30 odd years ago. It was a crisp Spring day in March and, out of the blue as if gently placed there from above by some benign deity, an almost mint-condition racing bike was discovered just lying out in front of the house. A mixture of confusion and restrained excitement descended over the family. Where did it come from? Can we keep it? Who does it belong to? Can we KEEP it? Was it stolen or lost? CAN we KEEP it? Will someone come by to collect it? CAN.WE.KEEP.IT???!

My parents decided to do what they always at least try to do, the right thing. So the bike was wheeled down to the local Garda station where it stood in solitary confinement whilst flyers were posted around the area to notify the owners of its location and how to collect it. Six months pass. My fresh-faced siblings have long forgotten about the mystery bike and its whereabouts. They are even unaware of the call from the Garda station to inform them no-one has come forward to claim it so the ancient legal statute of 'Finders Keepers' was about to kick in as the bike officially becomes the property of the young Morgan family. With that rarest of unbridled glee, the kind laced with pride, at being rewarded for doing the right thing my Dad and brother set at fixing up the loose edges of the bike. The brake pads, wheels and every bolt shone, as they were either replaced or given a generous rub of a cloth. Before too long it looked almost like new and was being giddily rolled down the garden path to be shown off as if it was a new born baby. With gusto my brother threw his leg over the crossbar and began racing up and down the road in between the odd slow victory circle with no hands to show off. And then a cloud appeared in the horizon. A cloud in the form of a car which drew closer and unexpectedly slowed to a stop beside my brother and his friends. A direct conversation began through the car window and was followed by a more heated exchange leading to an irate looking lady trouncing up the garden path of our house. When my Mam answered she was berated and shouted at until the reason became clear why the lady was so furious...

"Your boy stole our bike! He's a no good thief! We're taking it back right now!"

My Mam was a mixture of angry, confused and ultimately devastated. All the joy the bike had brought after doing the right thing and now it looked as though it was all being undone, with incredible vitriol too. My Dad arrived by her side and after much exasperation and explanation the only correct choice was to once again get the Gardai involved to sort things out. The call to the Garda station delivered the expected dreaded conclusion...

"...if the lady can confirm ownership we'll have to give it back to her unfortunately..."

No-one liked it but my folks were again compelled to do the right thing and obey. They sent my brother and a pal back down the road with the bike to deliver it to the owners' house. Unbeknownst to my folks at the time, the bike was ravenously stripped of every shiny part that the Morgan family had applied to it just days before. A few days later my Mam & Dad found out that by the time the bike made it back to its owner it had been quietly stripped of any extra parts they had added to it during its time with the family. It wasn't destroyed but my Dad's talent for understatement summed it up when he told me the bike was no longer roadworthy by the time it got 'home'. Under the circumstances the whole family agreed that too had been the right thing to do. A cheeky moral victory snatched from the jaws of a painful defeat.

But the cycling seed had been sown and my parents decided to recapture the excitement my brother had experienced just a few months later on a frosty Christmas morning. They had planned it all out with more than a little mischief. On Christmas morning he raced down the stairs daring not to dream of what the darkened living room might hold for him. Breathlessly he barged in and there it was. Placed delicately on the table in front of him was a brand new bicycle...pump. A solitary bicycle pump. His disbelief was eased unpleasantly by my Dad confirming that my brother now had permission to pump up the bald tyres of my father's old bike and cycle it any time he wanted, provided it wasn't already in use. The look on my brother's face, I'm told, said all he needed to say as he turned and trudged through the Venetian doors separating the living room from the dining room. And then he saw it. Gleaming, as if made solely from aluminium, his very own brand new bike. An altogether different kind of disbelief overcame him but this time it was overcome by the giggling of my parents as they hugged him close and said softly…

"Merry Christmas Kiddo"

Cheeky feckers, don't you think?! But here we are over three decades later still adding that little bit of mischievous magic to the unveiling of our own kids toys. There was a period in my young adulthood when Christmas was more a travail than a joy but I must confess not that between my wife and my two sons I am very much a born again Christmas-ian, if it is possible to be such a thing.

There are plenty of unavoidable 'reality checks' to come in the years ahead for the boys so for just a few years when they are truly susceptible to magic & wonder. So over the Christmas period in particular, we try and cram in as much as possible…

"Daddy has to go back to the Christmas forest and find the tree he left back last year and make sure it's grown big and strong again…"

Since last years tree actually dried out and died by January 1st, the bored teenager manning the Christmas tree section outside Woodies will have to provide the magic for Daddy while the boys stay at home digging out the decorations. Christmas officially starts when Ben in his Dad's arms places the over-sized glitter-speckled star atop the tree. Throughout the month of December the magic dust continues to layer a sprinkling coating of mystique across proceedings. With every visit to a grotto or yuletide song sung along to; the boys spend their time wide-eyed and smiling. Culminating on the afternoon of Christmas Eve when we all head out for a long walk in the park. It's always funny to see how many young kids are being escorted around the parks on the day with a view to being exhausted as quickly as possible thus ensuring and early and sleep-filled night. The best part is when Dad gets to be a little mischievous, staying behind to lock up as everyone heads to the car for the trip to the park. I stay behind to write a quick letter to the boys from Rudolph and place it carefully in the sitting room beside two sets of very special Christmas pyjama's he wants the boys to wear that night. When everyone arrives back home after a long stroll, just to make bed-time an even more appealing notion we watch as the boys open the door and we wait behind as they walk in. Ben captures the moment nicely...

"-What the heck?! Mom, Dad look Christmas pyjamas! Santa & Rudolph were here!"

We read out the letter which says Rudolph hopes they boys like their special pyjamas and they be sure to leave out cookies & milk for Santa; Carrots & water for the reindeer. The lads lap it up and are sound asleep before 7pm. We get the place organised so that, in the morning to their blissfully innocent minds, Father Christmas and his reindeer have been and gone and delivered all the presents they wished for and a few surprises too.

Now I fully realise how easy it is to see that as twee, corny and dumb. In the context of the world we live in today, where the swift cynical quip gains instant celebrity world, how can you not read the above and picture someone as naïve as say Ned Flanders? I can't defend or condone the level of saccharine sweetness in some of the things we do but the good news is I don't really have to. It doesn't bother us how 'gay' some cynical people might think it is. The only thing that matters is the imagery and wonder it creates in the minds of our two boys. And they love it. Someday they might read this and quiver with embarrassment. But at the same time they will maybe have girlfriends, jobs, mortgages and a whole load of other woes to deal with. For now, in this first few years when the have nothing but childish hope & innocence in them, we just want to indulge their imaginations as best we can before the weight of the world forces them to grow up. In return they have given us something we thought we had lost when we 'grew up'.

Put simply I now believe in Santy once again. No I haven't been into the gone off strawberry jam again, I actually do. Whether or not there is a guy on a sleigh who gets down every chimney on earth using only reindeer powered flight & wishful thinking is not the point. The point is what that time of year brings out in most if not all of us. Forget the shopping, that's just psychotic madness. It's Christmas Eve & Morning I'm talking about. The price of the presents are forgotten, the big blazing row in the Summer is a faded memory. For just a few hours everyone feels…something.

Something other than worried or depressed. And that comes from how much kids get into it. Whether they realise it or not it's something they pass on to us too. For nearly a whole month you look people in the eye and smile. You wish them goodwill and happy holidays whether you are drunk or not. You try those silly mischievous tricks with presents like my folks did to get an extra bit of excitement going. If all of that is because of the notion of an overweight, bearded man from Lapland flying around the world in one night delivering presents I am on board 100%. I even cut up the carrots just the way the reindeer like them!

We're not complete dreamers though don't worry. Like most parents we also use the venerable Santa as a bargaining tool to encourage as much good behaviour as possible along the way. Eating dinner, sharing toys, staying in bed at night all get attributed to deciding whether they are on the naughty or nice list. A lot of hay is made while the Santa-sun shines as it's the strongest negotiating time of the year for parents. The only problem is on the day after Christmas its back to the usual basic forms of child blackmail. Unfortunately it's a long way to Easter and the Bunny does carry as much clout as the big man in the red coat. Treats and toys definitely do work as an indispensible carrot to dangle in front of the kids. The only problem is which carrot to choose.

It's sometimes difficult to enjoy watching them play with today's toys without thinking about how much thought went into marketing them to you and your children. They were advertised, directly and indirectly, very cleverly to ensure you ended up with them in your living room.

Don't get me wrong I do love some of the toys myself and enjoy getting down on the floor to play with the boys as much as possible. Though most times they (already) think I'm way too uncool to play with. The thing that bugs me nowadays is the scale. It used to be just a singular toy. A doll, an action figure, Lego maybe even Mecanno like my Dad got all those years ago. But today no toy stands alone. Everything is a franchise. The kids want the toy because they've seen the book, TV show or the DVD. And whichever one of those media they have not seen yet will be next on the list because the range is endless. The toy now links with a book for bed time, the movie on the skybox and the DVD spin-off.

There are also the pyjamas, t-shirts & runners with the character emblazoned all over them. And that's just *one* character from *one* range. You will soon be asked for the lesser characters in the gang who also have all their own accessories and paraphernalia to go with them. Even better is the fact that most of them will only be the centre of attention for a matter of weeks. Inevitably, eventually they will lose their appeal and something new comes along with a completely new smorgasbord of characters to buy.

The entertainment and the actual toys are now inextricably linked together. On a rainy afternoon the boys will have the full cast of Toy Story spread across the room as they recreate their own version of the scenes playing out on the television in the corner. They are not even watching it but it is nonetheless a key factor in creating the illusion that these toys, these characters are more than just inanimate objects. I don't have a problem with the TV helping in that imaginative process as long as it's not the centre of attention leading to blank staring faces. The trouble is how expensive it is to satisfy the desire to have all the characters in all their various guises. They are neither cheap nor small in number. But we trade off other areas of our budget to deliver as much of them as we can because they simply give the boys so much healthy stimulating entertainment. If a little television in the right controlled doses helps fire their imagination to create and build things that's a bonus too. I know some parents think television is the devil and that's their choice. I've never seen the harm myself as long as it's not used as a stand-in parent every minute of the day. Besides I watched television constantly for nearly a decade as a teenager and I turned out perfectly Panasonic…I mean Sharp.

Thankfully the standard of television & films designed for children today is light years ahead of when I was young. All I had was Chitty Chitty Bang Bang which only served to scar me for life (if you don't remember, just skip forward to any scene involving the child-catcher). As it did any parent who was forced to sit through it with me. Today however the choice available to kids, via their parent's approval, is simply jaw-dropping in scale and is (mostly) high quality. The added benefit is that the really high-end programmes & movies are designed with the knowledge that parents have to suffer through them too. As a result they usually contain at least a few moments (if not more) that fly over the head of kids and keep adults relatively sane until we get our hands on the remote again. They do still trigger some unprofessional parenting behaviour though...

"Dad can I watch the Tinkerbell movie please?"

"(*Oh God no*) Eh sorry mister I think the DVD is gone missing, why don't we watch your Cars movie instead??"

"No here is the Tinkerbell DVD I found it, Now we can watch it together!"

"Ok...oh hang on look its all scratched it won't work, lets put on Cars instead"

"No Dad I want to watch Tinkerbell!"

"Ok Ok let me put in the disc....there we go, now I'll just press play..."

"NO DADDY THIS IS CARS I DON'T WANT TO WATCH THAT!"

"Ah sorry I must have put in the wrong disc. But sure its started no so we may as well watch it, here sit up with me"

"No, I'm going to play with my toys"

*"Ok well if you change your mind we can watch Cars together here...Ok buddy? Buddy?...(*I'm a terrible father...who is now watching a children's movie alone...still beats Tinkerbell though, Ka-Chow!!*)"*

In the months leading up to delivery, much like the epidural, the television is considered something that will only be used as a last resort. It sits conspicuously in the corner of the living room, seemingly relentless in its desire to hoover up everyone's interpersonal skills and attention. No way are you going to let that evil device consume the developing brain power of your child, no way! But jump ahead a couple of years and it will become an invaluable tool, a time-buyer if you will, for helping you get through many a difficult day. The benefit television can provide (yes I said it) is enhanced when used in a keenly struck balance between indoor & outdoor pursuits. Also, when stuck indoors, a balance between using their toys to create their own little imaginary world and having a little diversion time from the old radiation box in the corner. Ben for example will watch a scene play out on the TV screen and within minutes he has disappeared into his imagination on the other side of the room re-creating his own version of that scene with his toys. Sometimes if a character is missing he finds a way of using something else as a perfectly suitable substitute. One day for example he kept coming to Lucy asking for hair bobbins, one after another. Naturally my long dormant caveman gene kicked into high gear as I prepared to go into his room and have a frank talk about boys not wearing bobbins in their hair. When we peeked in to his room however we saw what he was actually doing. He was using the bobbins as rope to tie up his Buzz Lightyear for his interrogation by the bad guys, whom he had assembled in a semi-circle around the prisoner. This was, according to all the clever child psychologist people folk, a great developmental exercise for Ben as he created a world around him and filled it with his imagination. The seed for that creation was sown from that 'evil' television in the front room. In the right balance it's capable of doing a lot more good than harm. And yes, it also helps get you the odd five minutes of peace. On a rainy day, that can be hugely beneficial to keeping everyone sane and on speaking terms.

When it comes to entertainment another crucial factor that goes hand in hand with balance is content. Choosing which programs or movies match with your child's interest and your own parenting preferences is a difficult enough task on its own. But it also usually cause numerous arguments between you and your partner due to the differing opinions you both have on what is appropriate, fun or educational viewing. The good news is the quality of content and the sheer scale of choice available for children's entertainment is mid-boggling. The inevitable problem is they will not always agree with you as to what programme or movie is best for them to watch.

The amount of time and scientific research that goes into making most children's programming is very impressive. We are way beyond 'Bill & Ben the flowerpot men' here. Today there are not only programmes designed specifically for your child's exact stage of development but entire channels. The films produced today are mostly designed with some kind of decent 'be true to yourself' message that does no harm at all whilst also being intelligent enough to keep adults entertained at the same time. No easy feat. In comparison to the type of children's films I remember watching as a young boy I believe kids and parents are spoilt for choice. Plus there are significantly less murders of parental figures in them nowadays. I've lost count of how many times whilst watching the 'classic' animated films I had to use the phrase…

"Its ok, his Mommy is just asleep...on the ground...not breathing...(*panic whilst scrambling around for the remote*)"

But whether you like it or not, in the pursuit of parental supervision, you will end up an avid viewer of some very odd television programmes and movies. Some of which must have been conceived by the creators with the assistance of some expensive recreational drugs. It's one of two unwritten conditions you do not get told about before becoming a parent; 1) you will find yourself becoming far too aware of the lives of a variety of animated characters and puppets as you share in your child's entertainment and 2) you will find yourself having the most bizarre frequent conversations regarding the colour, consistency and odour of well, shite. It's one of the the strangest thing you barely notice. You dive off the path to avoid stepping in poo yet at least three times a day you willingly lift up a tiny person, rest their backside against your face and sniff to check if they have 'eliminated'. Parents really do lead a charmed life sometimes. However while there are few redeeming features to the poo situation at least the entertainment side of things does come with some positives. Since you will have to sit through the things your child watches too, the good news is some of them are actually quite bearable, some even enjoyable. Some unfortunately…not so much.

Myself and the boys have had some great movie experiences on those rainy days when there's not much else to do. In fact, I challenge any parent, especially Dads, to watch 'Finding Nemo' with their son beside them and not end up saying something affectionate to them at the end or even simply putting your arm around them as they squeeze your hand a little tighter. Just make sure it doesn't look like you've been choked up when the next adult walks into the room. I'm yet to manage that one myself. Then there are the other cold evenings before bed-time when the only thing they want to watch is Alvin & the Chipmunks, a collection of Mammals who very much push the boundaries of bearable. Ben also had a period where he was fascinated with a very popular show called Lazytown. Again a lot of positive scientific research apparently went into its creation and on average each series cost several million to produce. The driving theme of the show is that exercise is good and being a couch potato is bad which is perfectly laudable. The hero Sportacus, played by a real-life Olympian and world-renowned gymnast, spends most of each episode cart-wheeling and doing the splits across the screen. He performs these feats to the background soundtrack of cheesy-euro-dance-music reminiscent of The Vengaboys. He eats only fruit so at first glance we thought 'if he must watch something at least there is an inherently positive message in this one'. However the outcome once the show was over was like we had poured a bag of sugar into Ben's mouth and washed it down with a strawberry milkshake. He'd spend the next hour pole-vaulting off the coffee table with an apple in his hand. It never went close to his mouth unfortunately, that part he didn't fancy imitating. We swiftly started avoiding the programme like the plague, not that it was bad, it was just easier than forcing Ben to wear protective headgear for the afternoon. He gave out plenty but soon forgot about it which was great because aside from the impact on him watching the programme was a really good short-cut to a full frontal migraine for us.

Dougie took a long time to chisel out his own entertainment preferences and interests. As you have heard he has always been a very active child, that's putting it mildly. He entered the world at 100 miles an hour just 15 minutes after we walked in the front door of the hospital and has not slowed down much in the two years since. We were stumped because his high energy levels dwindled not much at all during out 'solid bedtime routine'. He would come out of the bath as if it was a cold shower, even more excited than when he went in. This was the opposite of what we were going for and naturally we started to panic about how we could maintain our routine of a peaceful bedtime around 7pm every night. Then one evening after his bath we stumbled into The Night Garden.

I have no idea how the research was conducted but the idea is that the show is designed to wind children *down* and prepare them physically and psychologically for bed. A noble creative notion but the actual look and feel of the programme is truly bizarre. Not in a bad way, just a little…weird. Okay, a *lot* weird! The bottom line is it effortlessly, almost subliminally, draws in both adults and kids to the point where they almost start to speak slower and yawn. It's wonderfully captivating yet utterly confusing. I still have no idea what it is actually about in conventional terms but it matters not. The important thing is that it fits in with our routine and almost guarantees us a peaceful parade of little men down the hall and into bed by the time the credits roll.

Having spent the day doing your best to ensure your child gets all the education, stimulation & fun that they can I think parents are entitled to a few hours to relax as adults. If a simple yet mind-warping little show beaming out from the 'evil' box in the corner helps them to dream sweetly and helps us put our feet up nice and early surely that's a good thing. Hell it's almost worth the price of the Sky subscription all on its own.

Be careful what you wish for though. A whole evening to relax as adults? You might find yourselves with a little bit too much *adult* time on your hands for your own good.

And just as everything was beginning to

settle down…

———————————————

Ten

That Difficult Second Album

" – Hey, remember we talked about having another baby the other night?"

"Yeah, about that, I nee-"

"I know, I know, I can tell what you're thinking and it's ok because I completely agree. We were getting ahead of ourselves and I don't think we are ready to face into all that again. The pregnancy, the labour, the night feeds...why don't we just focus on us for a while, doesn't that sound nice?"

"........I'm pregnant"

"Hey Wow, That's Great News, C'mere You!...(*ah bollox!*)"
-Gary, Dad of Three

The decision to 'go again' (or simply the discovery that you *are* going again without prior notice) and try baby number two is sometimes a tricky one. You've made it through the pregnancy, morning sickness and pointless bickering and come out the other side somehow still together. In addition you've managed to produce a little person beginning to do things for themselves too. You're catching up on your soaps, using your season ticket to big matches for the first time in ages and everyone is starting to get almost human quantities of sleep again. All is starting to settle down and you're even reconnecting with each other physically too. 'Reconnecting physically' is what the experts call it when you both remember you are actually a couple as well as parents. Usually what happens next is a romantic dinner, a few drinks and the kind of recklessly passionate sex that would make a dog in heat blush. And so, (4-6 minutes later) everyone is happy.

But one person will always be just a tiny bit happier with that than their partner is. As a result they can actively work very carefully to maintain the status quo, always ensuring the medicine cabinet is fully stocked with all required varieties of contraception. Meanwhile their other half is already beginning to ponder, sometimes even subconsciously, about the possibility of adding another name to the family team-sheet. The conversations that follow can vary wildly depending on how things went for both of you during the previous couple of years. You could be quite optimistic about parenting and have already taken a lot of positives from the first run at pregnancy. Alternatively you could have hung on for dear life by your finger nails throughout the rollercoaster ride and now just want to get back to normality. It's quite easy to identify who is who though. One of you is saying...

"- Could we afford it? We nearly tore each other apart the last time. It will be difficult to manage the budget. Remember how sick you where?"

And the other appears to not hear those concerns while jumping in with...

"- Just think of her with a little brother or sister, we have most of the stuff we need already, I think she would love a sibling...what do you think?"

If you are the former by the way you may as well forget it, it doesn't matter what you think, you will be having another baby shortly, Mazeltov! This dynamic should not be interpreted as a universal 'Dad saying no and Mom saying yes' in every scenario. It really is dictated by experiences of parenting thus far when it comes to planning the next phase of family development.

My own mother finds this whole family planning conundrum a considerably high-class problem. She and her peers did not have the option of discussing and considering the pros & cons of additional children. They got married and if they fancied having sex with the man they loved they invariably had a child 40 weeks later. That's good old fashioned Catholic family planning. My Mam shocked me when she summed up the experiences of married women just 40 short years ago. This is not necessarily her exact experience but the vast majority of women her age will confirm that it common practice at the time for them to seek guidance from a familiar place, the parish priest...

"Father, I need your help with something"

"Of course young lady what can I do for you?"

"Well, I have a sick little boy, my son, who needs all my attention so we cannot risk having another baby at the moment so...well, I am on my way to collect some contraception and I was hoping you could give me absolution before I start using it"

"No child, I cannot give you absolution from that sin"

"But, I can't care for my son and my husband and have another baby at the same time...please Father?"

"No, what you need to do is just go straight home and be a good wife to your husband, it sounds like he needs you to be a better wife than you have been to him lately"

"Oh....okay thank you Father"

"God bless and peace be with you"

Eight weeks later that woman found out she was pregnant. Peace was not something she saw a lot of for the next few decades.

Thankfully parents can be a little more discerning nowadays. That is by no means a guarantee of a joint decision however. Are you really both on the same page? Well as I said, a lot depends on how things have gone first time around. Permit me to continue the musical analogy used in the title of this chapter to elaborate. If you have a lead singer who has had a ball and been loved by all during the recent world tour he is obviously going to be counting the days until the band hits the road again. Unlike the drummer, who is swamped in routine thankless tasks and never gets so much as a single fan mail. He is considerably less likely to be itching to pack his bags next time around when a possible tour is mentioned. Of course if the drummer and singer get drunk one magical night and record what, at the time, sounds like a fantastic album then the decision becomes irrelevant. You're both going back on the road with that new album before you've even listened back to it and realised its not quite the masterpiece it seemed on that magical night.

In some cases it can even be driven by innocuous incidents of cuteness delivered by your first born child. You look and wonder at how precious your child is as he does his little dance or sings that song he likes and you both can't help but think;

"We've done it once, surely it would just be twice the enjoyment of what we're seeing right now...let's do it"

But what you unavoidably forget to add in to your calculation is that it's also twice the vomiting, bloating, fighting, screaming, pushing, tearing (see? That word has a whole new meaning now) and that's before you even get home to break the news to your little showstopper that their spotlight is no going to be shared, forever.

Ben pretty much had twenty straight months of our sole undivided attention for the most part. His room was his own and he had his run of the toy box any time he wanted. Every family activity was focused on him as was the video camera. We have hundreds of photos of Ben during his first year and a half or so; from every angle during all sorts of activities. Dougie on the other hand is only now starting to appear amidst the family photo collages. Though to be fair it's not entirely our fault. He was so active so early in his life that trying to take a picture of him was like trying to photograph

Bigfoot. A blurry limb here, a naked arse disappearing out of frame there, it was impossible.

But in comparison to his older sibling Dougie drew the short straw when it came to parental attention in his own first twenty months. There was just no time and no space for much one on one time. And when you add in to the mix Ben acting out any time Dougie required attention it got even more complicated. As soon as his younger brother would look to be fed or require changing Ben would coincidentally need help from us with something. At best that would be help putting his Mr. Potato Head toy together. At worst he would climb the highest piece of furniture he could find, just as we were attending to Dougie, so we had to leave what we were doing and discipline him.

Dougie was also a serious handful from the minute he arrived home. He cried at a pitch just short of what would be required to cause dogs in the local area to go deaf. And he vomited…a lot, usually just before bedtime too so it was not always easy to have the same kind of special moments with him that we shared with Ben. Dougie missed out on a lot of things that we took for granted with Ben. On the flipside however Dougie has something incredible that Ben did not and will never experience. Something that outweighs all the toys and solo Mom and Dad moments Ben ever had. Dougie has a big brother. Dougie has Ben.

From the day he arrived home Dougie has idolised Ben. Yes they fight and squabble very often, which siblings of any age don't. But with a bit of luck Dougie will never need to worry about facing anything alone for the rest of his life. And neither will Ben because even when we are long gone, shuffled off into the afterlife they will have each other. They may not like each other but they will have each other nonetheless. Whether or not they will have another sibling to develop a fractured but meaningful long term bond with is a question we do not know the answer to yet. With more space, more money the answer may well be yes. But the clock is ticking and if we wait until economic conditions improve to the point where we have the required space and money to adequately support expanding the family it may be too late. If my Dad were here he would surely chime in with a solid...

"Sure see what happens, play it by ear and don't be worrying about things you can't control"

He'd make a brutal fortune-teller but he has a point. So we shall see wait for now and not fear what lies ahead of us in the next few years. For now we have enough to keep us occupied making sure we are doing the best we can for Ben and Dougie to give them the best chance of happy and successful lives.

Considering the weight of that responsibility for a moment reminds me of how we started this little journey through Parenthood. That most daunting, recurring and complicated of questions which stares back at every parent when they look in the mirror…Am I a Good Parent?

The inconvenient truth of the matter is that you will probably never know for sure. How do you define success as a parent anyway? An adult son or daughter who is emotionally sound and an incredibly popular figure among her peers? What if the trade-off was that she had no concept of managing money and so ended up in huge debt and living off the land with a new age hippy commune? They are happy so is that success? Or is it when your child turns forty-five and is half way through a steady predictable career in a public service job which he will never be at risk of losing. He will never have to worry about money or bills for the rest of his life. But he lives alone and has no interest in friends or meeting a partner, ever...See? Success is not only difficult to achieve its also nearly impossible to define. But surely you can reach a point where you can determine that you have done more things right than wrong and therefore you can call yourself a good parent...Yes? Nope. It's not that simple because you don't get to make that call. Neither do the nosey neighbours behind their lace curtains. It's not the business of the parents who sneer at you from across the playground judging you from afar. It's not for social workers, government officials or even the clergy to tell you that you have done a good job as a parent. No, that judgement can only come from one place. Your children.

One day many years from now when they are mature enough to appreciate and understand what you have done for them, and how you have done it, they will tell you what the think. They may not say it aloud but they will definitely show you in some way. Their acknowledgement may coincide with the arrival of their own children which, as I have found, sheds new light on how much unseen work and worrying a parent goes through.

You want proof? Well here you go. I had two good parents. I'm lucky to still have them and that is something I appreciate every day. They did plenty of good stuff I have no recollection of like because I was only a baby but I am here today so that in itself is proof they put the hard graft in. There is even more that they gave me that I thankfully do remember. They made me laugh, kept me safe, taught me right from wrong with a firm hand and to respect those around me at all times. They have adopted my wife as if she was their own daughter and proved wonderful grandparents to my children. There is no gratitude I could offer them that would ever truly balance my account with them but if they are reading this I hope this admission of their good work will serve as some compensation for the years of work they put in to me. I can only hope that I make them proud to see me at least trying to put in the same shift with my own children. I think I do. But whether that is enough for me to one day be reading a note of similar sentiment from my two sons is a complete mystery. My wife and I, actually all parents, don't know from one day to the next if what we are doing is definitely the right thing for our kids. We may not find out for many years, if we ever find out at all. You can only do what you feel is right and then simply cross your fingers it all turns out for the best in the end.

There is a good chance however that if you are reading this book then you do care about the responsibility you have and that is 90%

of the battle. The other 10% is usually blind luck. Sometimes those figures can actually be reversed too. But if any of these little stories have struck a chord with you then there is a strong chance that like me you come from good stock. And if that is true then so do your kids so they will do just fine and so will you.

For now our brief journey through Parenthood has reached its end. There is more to tell including school gate politics, sibling rivalries and lots of puppies. But those my dear friends are stories for another book and another day...

To Be Continued

In

Parenthood; Rising Sons

6768474R00151

Printed in Great Britain
by Amazon.co.uk, Ltd.,
Marston Gate.